BREAKING RANKS:
Changing *an* American INSTITUTION

A Report of the National Association of Secondary School Principals in partnership with the Carnegie Foundation for the Advancement of Teaching on the high school of the 21st century.

ACKNOWLEDGMENT

The National Association of Secondary School Principals is indebted to the Commissioners for their time, dedication, and vision. The uniqueness of the practitioners' perspective has resulted in powerful recommendations for programs and practices that will enable educators in our nation's high schools to prepare students for the 21st century.

NASSP is most grateful to Gene I. Maeroff, Senior Fellow, Carnegie Foundation for the Advancement of Teaching, for his writing skills and ability to help the Commission bring focus and clarity to the recommendations. His dedication of time, patience, and persistence in compiling all the ideas from the many hours of deliberation into the development of this report have been exemplary.

In addition, NASSP would like to recognize all the dedicated staff members who provided support for the Commissioners' work. Their assistance was invaluable in ensuring the Commission's duties were fulfilled in a timely and efficient manner.

NASSP Board of Directors 1995-1996

President: E. Don Brown, Principal, L.D. Bell HS, Hurst, Tex.

President-Elect: H. Michael Brown, Principal, Hope HS, Hope, Ark.

James M. Aseltine, Principal, Irving A. Robbins MS, Farmington, Conn.

Robert A. Baines, Principal, Manchester West HS, Manchester, N.H.

Thomas D. Beattie, Superintendent, Pulaski SD, Pulaski, Wis.

A. Keith Bridges, Principal, Clinton HS, Clinton, S.C.

Kirk A. Brower, Principal, Star Valley HS, Afton, Wyo.

Alfred D. DiEmedio, Principal, Smyrna HS, Smyrna, Del.

Thomas R. Drake, Principal, Des Moines Lincoln HS, Des Moines, Iowa

Douglas A. Fagan, Principal, Solon HS, Solon, Ohio

Patricia Haller, Principal, Dayton HS, Dayton, Nev.

Eugene S. Haydock, Principal, Fredonia HS, Fredonia, Kans.

John Lewis, Principal, Rainier MS, Rainier, Oreg.

J. Patrick Mahon, Principal, Meadowcreek HS, Norcross, Ga.

John C. Osteen, Principal, Lake Taylor HS, Norfolk, Va.

W. Cecil Short, Principal, William Wirt MS, Riverdale, Md.

Gary F. Smyly, Principal, Columbia HS, Columbia, Miss.

Curt Voight, Principal, South MS, Rapid City, S. Dak.

Donald A. Wallace, Principal, Cheyenne Mountain Jr. HS, Colorado Springs, Colo.

Brenda Weber, Assistant Principal, Evansville North HS, Evansville, Ind.

Timothy J. Dyer, Executive Director

Thomas F. Koerner, Deputy Executive Director

Ronald D. Baird, Associate Deputy Executive Director for Human Resources and Financial Services

Kathleen A. DeFloria, Associate Executive Director, Corporate Partnerships

John A. Lammel, Director of High School Services

Robert Mahaffey, Director of Communications

Patricia Lucas George, Associate Director of Publications

Debra Roth, Associate Director of Public Relations

Eugenia Cooper Potter, Technical Editor

In Dedication
DR. ERNEST L. BOYER AND THE NATION'S YOUTH

This report is dedicated to the memory of Dr. Ernest L. Boyer and to the nation's youth, who were the beneficiaries of his distinguished career in education. It is natural and fitting in light of Dr. Boyer's many contributions to young people that they share this dedication. Most recently as president of the Carnegie Foundation for the Advancement of Teaching and earlier as U.S. Commissioner of Education and before that as chancellor of the State University of New York, Dr. Boyer shaped and influenced policies and practices that will affect the nation's youth for generations to come.

He readily lent his support to this report and proposed that it be the product of the deliberations of practitioners, not of high officials whose day-to-day lives are removed from the schools. And so, from the very beginning, Dr. Boyer provided inspiration for the report. He even addressed the members of the Commission when they assembled for their first meeting on a bright Sunday morning in Princeton in the spring of 1994.

Dr. Boyer did not live long enough to see the final product of the Commission's work, but he encouraged the process and provided the financial and intellectual support of the Carnegie Foundation for the Advancement of Teaching. Exactly two weeks before his death, Dr. Boyer reviewed a nearly completed copy of the manuscript and offered suggestions for changes that are reflected in this document. He wrote many important reports of his own during his tenure as head of Carnegie, including *High School: A Report on Secondary Education in America*. While this new report cannot claim to be one of his, it nevertheless owes its very existence to him and to the Carnegie Foundation. If, as a result of the influence of this report, the nation's youth end up better educated in their high schools that outcome will be another of Ernie Boyer's legacies. ∎

PREFACE

"The time has come, Tim." With these words spoken by Ernie Boyer to me in the East Room of the White House at a reception to honor health programs for our nation's children we concluded that it was time and necessary for a serious review of the American high school. We had been conversing for nearly a year prior to this chance meeting. A definitive study of the key elements essential to reform one of the most venerable institutions in our society was necessary and paramount. It had not been done in many years and there had been no serious treatment since *High School: A Report on Secondary Education in America* was completed in 1983.

What attracted both of us to this important work was the abiding interest and commitment of the Carnegie Foundation for the Advancement of Teaching and the National Association of Secondary School Principals to providing educators with the best thinking possible, with a mechanism by which these ideas, thoughts, and reflections could be disseminated to the widest audience for ultimate implementation. Carnegie brought a rich array of scholarly research dating back decades concerning students and teachers and the fundamentals of how we as humans learn and use knowledge. NASSP, the preeminent organization of secondary administrators, could contribute much theory from its rich research base and from the 80 years of experiences of its thousands of members. But, most important, NASSP could institutionalize these findings and herald its message for decades.

Together, Carnegie and NASSP could unleash a powerful tool focused on the reform of the American high school and make it available to every high school in this nation. Dissemination could involve workshops, seminars, models, grassroots action plans by teachers, and principals taking the recommendations contained in this work and making them reality. Literally, every high school in this United States could and, we hope, will be affected by this undertaking.

By working together NASSP can guarantee for decades to come serious attention to the recommendations contained in *Breaking Ranks* along with ongoing follow-ups to determine successes and to evaluate changing times that may very well require alterations and adjustments as circumstances dictate.

This partnership was ideal. Accordingly, we began the work of putting together a national Commission composed exclusively of practitioners — a radical departure for Carnegie and NASSP in the way we have studied and conducted research projects. We dedicated ourselves to finding the very best practicing principals who daily dedicate their lives to the education of young adolescents and who know better than anyone the complexities, difficulties, and challenges associated with leading a modern American high school. Included on our Commission were eight principals, an assistant principal, two teachers, and two students, along with a central office administrator, two professors from institutions of higher learning, a senior fellow of the Carnegie Foundation for the Advancement of Teaching, and senior staff members of the National Association of Secondary School Principals.

The more than 80 recommendations are the result of the work of Commissioners with a wide and varied background who possess extensive scholarly knowledge and understanding of the skills necessary to implement change and who possess the ethical and moral underpinnings essential in leadership. The work lasted for over two years and their painstaking labors clearly reflected a broad understanding of what is necessary in order to improve the quality of education and prepare for the high school of the next millennium.

These recommendations are appropriate and applicable whether you are a private school, a public school, a voucher, charter, or any other type of school organization the local community chooses. These are recommendations for those who are seriously interested in the welfare of youth and their preparation for a productive and happy life following adolescence and graduation from high school.

High schools are complex and diverse institutions in this country. They are, in our society, an absolute necessity if you are to be successful at adult undertakings. Graduation from a high school in America is the entrance to adult life. In an ever-changing global environment where interdependency abounds the best and highest quality of education is a necessity no longer reserved for the few, but demanded for all. Any other course of action shall doom our future generations and nation to a third-class status.

We understand ever so clearly that in a democratic society the words of Thomas Jefferson ring resolute when he observed:

> "If a nation expects to be ignorant and free, in a state of civilization, it expects what never was and never will be."

The work of schooling is the most important work of a free, orderly democratic society. Absent it, you are enslaved.

The recommendations contained in this report are thoughtful, provocative and, most important, challenging. It will take great ingenuity, genius, and creativity to implement all of them. But this work must be done. We need the very best principals, teachers, and community leaders in order for our students to thrive in an ever dynamic nation and world.

There must be consistency and stability of leadership in our schools, particularly if any individual school is serious about the implementation of these recommendations. The words of T.E. Lawrence in his *Seven Pillars of Wisdom* ring when we think of the work that must be done by those who read this study and begin the arduous work of executing it:

> "All men dream: but not equally. Those who dream by night in the dusty recesses of their mind wake in the day to find that it was vanity: but the dreamers of the day are dangerous men, for they may act their dream with open eyes, to make it possible."

The Commission did not find a silver bullet, a panacea, an activity, a function that had never been thought of before, that had never been tried anywhere. The Commissioners' work is a series of recommendations that speaks to those who are committed to reform, the best thinking, knowledge, and skills currently available. It is a blueprint containing the ingredients that will make modern schooling work. These are the benchmarks of the future for this valiant institution called the American high school.

preface

There are many themes throughout this work, but if one theme could be extracted that is overarching and paramount, it is a message that the high school of the 21st century must be much more student-centered and above all much more personalized in programs, support services, and intellectual rigor. These seven recommendations are illustrative of what we envision: Every student will have a personal adult advocate; the Carnegie unit must be replaced or redefined; student anonymity must be banished; teachers should meet no more than 90 students per day; every student should have a Personal Plan of Progress; imaginative flexible scheduling must be the order of the day; every principal and teacher will have a Personal Learning Plan.

To make these recommendations work and the many others contained herein, we shall surely need "dreamers of the day"!

William Shakespeare 400 years ago recognized the need for leaders to seize the moments when they present themselves. The advice of Brutus to Cassius in *Julius Caesar* captures the moment we now have at hand:

"There is a tide in the affairs of men Which, taken at the flood, leads on to fortune; Omitted, all the voyage of their life Is bound in shallows and in miseries. On such a full sea are we now afloat, And we must take the current when it serves Or lose our ventures."

This is a great and glorious land, worthy of the very highest performance from its youth. In a time of national and international crises, America has always risen to the occasion. It has always taken the "flood... on to fortune." The work contained herein demands no less — in fact, our very future depends on how well we meet this task. ■

Timothy J. Dyer
Executive Director
National Association of
Secondary School Principals

Commission on the Restructuring of the American High School

Rupert J. Asuncion
Principal
Amos Alonzo Stagg H.S.
Stockton, CA

Frank J. Cody
Headmaster
Woodside Priory School
Portola Valley, CA

Curtis S. Collins, Jr.
Principal
Dennis-Yarmouth Reg. H.S.
South Yarmouth, MA

Esther J. Cox
Principal
M. L. King Jr. Career Center
Anchorage, AK

John C. Daresh
Professor
Department of Educational Leadership
and Foundations
Illinois State University
Normal, IL

Timothy J. Dyer
Executive Director
NASSP
Reston, VA

Alice B. Foster
Teacher
Mathematics
Millard North H.S.
Omaha, NE

Pat S. Graff
Teacher
Journalism/English
La Cueva H.S.
Albuquerque, NM

Marilyn Hohmann
Principal
Fairdale H.S.
1001 Fairdale Road
Fairdale, KY

David S. Hottenstein
Principal
Hatboro-Horsham Senior H.S.
Horsham, PA

John M. Jenkins
Professor
College of Education
University of Florida
Gainesville, FL

Laurel Martin Kanthak
Associate Executive Director
NASSP
Reston, VA

Thomas F. Koerner
Deputy Executive Director
NASSP
Reston, VA

John A. Lammel
Director, High School Services
NASSP
Reston, VA

Sidney Martin, III
Student
J.O. Johnson H.S.
Huntsville, AL

Charles E. Mingo
Principal
DuSable H.S.
Chicago, IL

Noreen M. Nilan
Student
Pompesaug Regional H.S.
Southbury, CT

James Sheehan
Assistant Principal
John I. Leonard Community H.S.
Lake Worth, FL

Georgina M. Takemoto
Deputy Superintendent
Fresno Unified School District
Education Center
Fresno, CA

Tim Westerberg
Principal
Littleton H.S.
Littleton, CO

Gene I. Maeroff, *Staff Writer*
Senior Fellow
Carnegie Foundation for the
Advancement of Teaching
Princeton, NJ

Table of Contents

PROLOGUE: WHAT MAKES THIS REPORT SPECIAL

Many have had their say about how to improve America's high schools—governors, legislators, policymakers, scholars from higher education, members of professional disciplinary associations, editorial writers, and a host of independent authors. Now, we believe, the time has come for those mainly responsible for the day-to-day operations of high schools to lay out their plans for educational reform. Thus, this report, unlike those previously issued, embodies a vision developed primarily by high school principals. It draws strength and authority from the fact that it arises from the inside and does not descend on high schools from the outside.

In the end, practitioners must carry the weight of the effort when it comes to high school renewal. Those who have sat in the principal's office have the best overview of what it takes to make high schools better. Their jobs require that they involve themselves in the instructional program, supervise and evaluate teachers, interact with parents, work with students, deal with the central administration, and in some places, oversee budgets and governance. In other words, they know what is practical and what is impractical. They are familiar with the challenges and the obstacles.

This report is unencumbered by politics or ideology. The driving force behind each recommendation is the single-minded consideration of what is best for the education of the country's teenagers, the life blood of the nation, as they are poised on the brink of adulthood. The Commission that formulated these proposals included principals, other administrators, and teachers; it also was one of the few panels of its kind to have students as members. The document is grounded in the experiences of those most profoundly involved in the American high school.

Lending additional significance to the words on these pages is the sponsorship of the National Association of Secondary School Principals, a membership organization that stands ready to launch a movement to implement the recommendations. Other reports offering proposals for school renewal have arrived like bolts of thunder unleashed by Zeus, briefly incandescent but quickly fading from view. In this instance, however, the secondary school principals group will work in the months and years ahead to illuminate a set of recommendations meant to carry high schools into the next century.

The report, more than two years in the making, is the beginning, not the end, of a process that will endure for the rest of this decade and into the next to restructure high schools in ways that will contribute to the academic success—and, ultimately, the success in life—of young Americans.

> The driving force behind each recommendation is the single-minded consideration of what is best for the education of the country's teenagers, the life blood of the nation, as they are poised on the brink of adulthood.

The National Association of Secondary School Principals in releasing this document commits itself to remain involved for the long haul. Few other reports on educational reform have had the leverage for change that the principals provide for this report. We realize that implementation of the recommendations will be difficult and complicated. We hope, however, that the report will serve as a template for examining existing policies and practices and that it will stir action when and where needed.

Therefore, these pages constitute a canvas on which we paint the broad brush strokes of high school reform; superintendents, school board members, principals, teachers, students, parents, and other members of high school communities around the country must fill in the details that fit their particular circumstances. No document of this sort can hope to serve as more than a manifesto for

action. Whatever steps they take, those who respond to the urgings of the Commission must be willing to depart from the status quo where appropriate. The very title of the report, *Breaking Ranks*, conveys a recognition that old ways that no longer work must yield to change. The changes should be guided by a sense of purpose.

What goals ought today's high schools to embrace? This question might be answered in hundreds of different ways. Certain themes, however, are apt to appear and reappear on any short list of the purposes of high schools. These nine purposes represent our vision for this nation's high schools and for the recommendations set forth in this report:

I. High school is, above all else, a learning community and each school must commit itself to expecting demonstrated academic achievement for every student in accord with standards that can stand up to national scrutiny.

II. High school must function as a transitional experience, getting each student ready for the next stage of life, whatever it may be for that individual, with the understanding that, ultimately, each person needs to earn a living.

III. High school must be a gateway to multiple options.

IV. High school must prepare each student to be a life-long learner.

V. High school must provide an underpinning for good citizenship and for full participation in the life of a democracy.

VI. High school must play a role in the personal development of young people as social beings who have needs beyond those that are strictly academic.

VII. High school must lay a foundation for students to be able to participate comfortably in an increasingly technological society.

VIII. High school must equip young people for life in a country and a world in which interdependency will link their destiny to that of others, however different those others may be from them.

IX. High school must be an institution that unabashedly advocates in behalf of young people. ■

Introduction
THOUGHTS FOR A HIGH SCHOOL IN A CHANGING WORLD

High school lays the foundation for what Americans become, and what Americans become shapes the high school that serves succeeding generations. Now, buffeted by powerful and unsettling winds, both the high school and the country are searching for stability and renewal. As a pivotal institution in the lives of young people, the high school can serve as a linchpin in efforts to improve the American condition, touching the lives of almost every teenager and, consequently, contributing to the betterment of the country.

Powerful transformations in values and behavior, in expectations and rewards, and even in the family itself render it essential that the high school reevaluate its purposes and functions, just as the society around it struggles to come to terms with the ramifications of these same changes. Almost one-third of all the children in the country under the age of 18 do not live with both parents.[1] One of five children lives in poverty.[2] And tens of thousands of high school students are presumably among the more than a half-million teenagers who deliver babies each year.[3] Furthermore, the job market has shifted decisively away from those who do not care sufficiently about education to get enough of it. All too many young people, however, do not comprehend the dire consequences of not using their time in school to productive advantage.

High schools must make it part of their mission to help young people understand that life without the intellectual tools for fully participating in the marketplace constitutes a sentence to likely destitution. A global economy leaves few places for Americans without adequate skills because the world is filled with those who will labor for wages for which few in this country could afford to work. Even the college-educated must take cognizance of their counterparts in other countries. Studies showing that students in the United States lag behind those in competing countries underscore the folly of clinging to the status quo.[4]

3

introduction

Students spend their mid-teens in high school, a relatively brief but highly formative period. They are, as adolescents, mostly in thrall to a larger society that exerts tremendous pressures on them. High school serves the young best by encouraging them to acquire the wherewithal for the next phase of their lives. They depart high school for a wide range of activities—jobs, the military, homemaking, technical school, community college, four-year college—and the diversity of these destinations indicates the importance of individualizing education. Their interests and ambitions differ greatly. The amount of reinforcement that they get from their families varies enormously. In addition to the common agenda, each student needs something different from high school. Yet, the separate experiences of each student must amount to a proper prelude for what comes next.

The country is diminished to the extent that any high school fails to provide all that it might for every student. We are, after all is said and done, one nation with a shared destiny. In a sense, high schools resemble boats afloat on a common sea, rising and falling together with the same tides. A young person who grows into adulthood unequipped to reach his or her full potential will possess neither the knowledge nor the will to contribute to making this a better society. The American high school, as an anvil upon which the nation forges its strength, must accept part of the blame for the troubles that surround it, having neglected to fulfill its duty to develop citizens who can assume their rightful place in a democracy with a free-market economy.

Many high schools face the prospect of diminished relevance in a future in which time and space, as traditionally used in education, will exert dwindling influence on the ability to deliver learning. Nevertheless, high schools continue to go about their business in ways that sometimes bear startling resemblance to the flawed practices of the past. Students pursue their education largely in traditional classroom settings, taught by teachers who stand before row upon row of desks. Mostly, these teachers lecture at students, whose main participation in class is limited to terse answers to fact-seeking questions. High schools persist in organizing instruction subject by subject with little effort to integrate knowledge. Learning continues to be dispensed in tidy 50-minute segments, as if anything worth knowing can be trimmed to fit a precise time frame in the manner that Procrustes accommodated weary travelers in his one-size-fits-all guest bed.

During much of this century, reformers sought to shut small high schools and herd youngsters into ever-larger schools that styled themselves after the factory model. Experts perceived bigness as a sine qua non of excellence. This paradigm, with its vast array of offerings, represented the epitome of educational progress. But students are not pieces on an assembly line and knowledge is not an inert commodity to pour into vessels like soft drink syrup in a bottling plant. The impersonal nature of high school leaves too many youngsters alienated from the learning process.

> ## A young person who grows into adulthood unequipped to reach his or her full potential will possess neither the knowledge nor the will to contribute to making this a better society.

High school stands at a juncture at which the students are perhaps most difficult to engage. The schools, however, predicate their programs on the idea that students will follow prescribed routines and will value the education that the institutions offer. This probably should not have been assumed in the past and it certainly should not be assumed about the very different teenagers of today. In yesterday's America, where the marketplace had a multitude of decently paying jobs for relatively unskilled labor, those who did not accord importance to education and even those who did not complete high school could at least find gainful employment, but today only the educated are apt to seize the future.

The cause of reform is hobbled by the inclination of educational institutions to resist substantial change. The rituals of high school, whatever their shortcomings, appeal to many people who suspect that substantial reform would undo the essence of teenhood. David F. Donavel, reflecting on the failure of restructuring in the high school in Massachusetts in which he worked as an English teacher, said: "The school, especially the high school, is nothing if not traditional and so has become the means by which people in our culture come to know who they are. Thus, any attempt at change violates our sense of who we are."[5] What passes as change is frequently no more than tinkering around the edges. *Plus ça change, plus c'est la même chose.* And so it is with America's high schools: The more they change, the more things seem to remain the same. It is not by accident that this report titles itself *Breaking Ranks*.

We believe that improvement requires high schools to alter themselves and so we present this vision of the future as one that preserves what is best while unapologetically offering new initiatives. Six main themes thread their way through the pages of this report, emphasizing that better education depends on personalizing the high school experience for students, lending coherency to their education, organizing time differently, using technology at every opportune point, revitalizing the ongoing professional education of teachers and administrators, and enhancing leadership at every level at which it can affect teaching and learning:

Personalization—High schools must break into units of no more than 600 students so that teachers and students can get to know each other better. Then, teachers should use a variety of instructional strategies that accommodate individual learning styles and engage students. This will be helped by every student having a Personal Adult Advocate and a Personal Plan for Progress.

Coherency—High schools should be clear about the essentials that students must learn to graduate. Disciplinary departments should be reorganized so that subjects are more closely linked and schools should align what they teach with what they test. In the end, learning must make sense to students in terms of the real world and the application of what they know.

Time—Teaching and learning need room for flexibility. High schools must abandon or revise the Carnegie unit so that they no longer equate seat time with learning. Furthermore, schools should operate 12 months a year and full-time teachers should not be responsible for more than 90 students a term so that they can give more attention to individual students.

Technology—High schools must develop a long-term plan for using computers, CD-ROMs, videodiscs, and other technologies in all aspects of teaching and learning. Toward this end, each high school must have a technology resource person to consult with and assist the staff. The curriculum should be conveyed through technology and teaching strategies should employ technology wherever appropriate.

The country is diminished to the extent that any high school fails to provide all that it might for every student.

Professional Development—Educators cannot improve high schools without the proper preparation to take on new roles and responsibilities. Their education in teacher colleges should equip them for changing demands in teaching and learning, and continuing inservice education must have a valued place in their day-to-day professional lives once they are on the job. Each educator in the school, including the principal, should have a Personal Learning Plan.

Leadership—Good intentions will come to naught unless people step forward to lead high schools into the future that is envisioned on these pages. Leadership in each high school must begin with the principal, but must include teachers, students, parents, school board members, the superintendent, and community residents who contribute to making schools better.

We understand that every student cannot be brilliant. Each student, however, can enjoy a measure of success on his or her own terms that represents solid achievement and genuine accomplishment in completing substantial and meaningful academic work. High schools must reformulate themselves in ways that lead to success for all students willing to put forth the effort. Teachers must prepare themselves to take on the challenge of lifting the learning levels of students whose failures have been lamented but accepted. Right now, it is a given that some students will learn and some will not. High schools tend to let everyone squeeze by—even most of those who are actually learning very little of an academic nature—as if moving on a conveyor belt. But the reality of American education is that some students are embarked upon a trip to nowhere.

introduction

Profound disparities exist among high schools and we do not pretend that all high schools are equally in need of improvement. In fact, without change, some high schools across the United States would continue to serve students more or less adequately. The problem, however, is that almost all high schools, even the best, are not all they could be. And certainly the worst high schools are in dire need of improvement. Leaving those at the bottom as they are would be to continue to place a significant portion of American youth at great peril.

As a complex institution, the high school comprises many interlocking parts. Alter one element and you affect others. Thus, the recommendations that we offer on the following pages are best viewed as a series of connected proposals that in many instances depend on implementation in one area for success in another. They flow from the purposes that we have enunciated. Piecemeal change may lead to some positive results, but it is not apt to be as effective as efforts that reach into the various parts of the system, in other words, systemic reform. High schools need more than tinkering.

We offer our proposals in three sections. First come the **priorities for renewal**, the recommendations affecting the individual elements that form the framework around which the high school should construct itself—curriculum, instructional strategies, school environment, technology, organization and time, and assessment and accountability. Second, we present recommendations dealing with the **web of support** that holds together the framework. These components lend strength or weakness to the overall structure. In this regard, we list professional development, diversity, governance, resources, ties to higher education, and relationships. Finally, the third section, brief but crucial, deals with **leadership**, the critical element without which little is likely to happen to improve high schools. ■

PRIORITIES FOR RENEWAL

The central aspects of teaching and learning must provide the focus for high school reform. The curriculum, instructional strategies, the school environment, the use of technology as a tool of learning, the ways in which the school organizes itself and how it uses time, and assessment and accountability directly determine the quality of schooling. These factors affect students in ways that promote or deter the pursuit of excellence. We want to emphasize at the outset of this report that we reject the idea of change without commensurate concern for high academic standards.

What does this mean in practice? It means that high schools must offer students a curriculum of substance, courses that require students to do serious work. It means that teachers use instructional strategies that engage students and make them part of the learning process. It means that each school must ensure that students have a climate supportive of teaching and learning, a setting in which academics are honored and distractions that interfere with serious purpose are not tolerated. It means that the school shuns frivolous uses of technology in favor of uses that enhance the quality of teaching and learning. It means that schools alter organization and time only in ways favorable to the maintenance of high standards. And, finally, it means that the chief aim of assessment ought to be to help students lift the quality of their work and that accountability certifies the integrity of the entire effort in teaching and learning.

Let no one doubt that the nation has had enough of shoddy academic standards and of high school programs that prepare students inadequately. Almost half of Americans (47 percent) say they do not believe that a high school diploma guarantees that a student has learned the basics.[6] Furthermore, 84 percent of the respondents to the 1995 Gallup Poll on public schools favored "higher standards than are now required in math, English, history, and science in order to graduate from high school."[7] More concern with standards will reassure a public that has grown dubious about the quality of a high school education in the United States. The nation can take justifiable pride in its commitment to universal elementary and secondary schooling, but this great achievement fades in significance when people believe that it has been attained at the expense of excellence. ■

The core of
the high school
curriculum must
offer both the
substance and the
practicality to
prepare students
for an uncertain
future. The curricu-
lum should resist
artificiality and strive
to meet individual
needs without
compromising
larger goals.

frameworks

chapter one
CURRICULUM
Offering Essential Knowledge, Integrating It, and Making Connections to Real Life

1. Each high school community will identify a set of essential learnings—above all, in literature and language, mathematics, social studies, science, and the arts—in which students must demonstrate achievement in order to graduate.

2. The high school will integrate its curriculum to the extent possible and emphasize depth over breadth of coverage.

3. Teachers will design work for students that is of high enough quality to engage them, cause them to persist, and, when successfully completed, result in their satisfaction and their acquisition of learnings, skills, and abilities valued by society.

4. The content of the curriculum, where practical, will connect itself to real-life applications of knowledge and skills to help students link their education to the future.

5. Assessment of student learning will align itself with the curriculum so that students' progress is measured by what is taught.

6. Each student will have a Personal Plan for Progress to ensure that the high school takes individual needs into consideration and to allow students, within reasonable parameters, to design their own methods for learning in an effort to meet high standards.

7. The high school will promote cocurricular activities as integral to an education, providing opportunities for all students that support and extend academic learning.

8. A high school will reach out to the elementary and middle level schools from which it draws students to help those schools understand what kind of foundation students need for success in high school and to respond to the needs of the lower schools for policies at the high school that reinforce earlier education.

articulation

1. Each high school community will identify a set of essential learnings—above all, in literature and language, mathematics, social studies, science, and the arts—in which students must demonstrate achievement in order to graduate.

High schools from Wyoming to Alabama should end the confusion about what a diploma represents. They can do this by clarifying what they expect of their graduates and then building a curriculum around the essential learnings that they have identified. In specifying that students study literature and language, mathematics, social studies, science, and the arts, we do not intend to imply that high schools should shun other areas of knowledge. We believe, though, that high schools must set priorities. Much room exists in a well-conceived high school curriculum for students to pursue, in addition to the core courses, foreign languages, technology, physical education, and a host of other subjects, individually and in an integrated format.

> High school graduates ought to be the beneficiaries of the contributions of the many people around them who end up sharing a stake in the students' success.

The federal government's Goals 2000: Educate America Act decrees that students will leave fourth, eighth, and twelfth grades having shown competency in English, mathematics, science, foreign languages, civics and government, economics, arts, history, and geography. Students should feel the impact as they enter and leave high school. In too many instances, this nation's high schools provide students with watered-down courses devoid of substance, the equivalent of intellectual cotton candy. Americans can no longer tolerate this practice. Students must know that schools will offer them purposeful studies, essential to an educated individual, and expect them to do real work.

As a step toward making academic studies more significant, high schools should spell out what students must know and be able to do with knowledge and skills. They can find some assistance in the guidelines developed by national organizations representing the various disciplines. Whatever sources the high schools draw upon, they should end up with standards that incorporate firm expectations of accomplishment. Someone who earns a diploma certainly ought to possess the ability to think critically and reason well. A senior might demonstrate this ability in English, for instance, by reading complex material and showing an understanding of the text, extracting meaning, analyzing and judging the quality and plausibility of the material, and offering evidence to support his or her judgments. This might be done by critiquing the arguments presented in columns on the op-ed pages of, say, the *New York Times* or the *Wall Street Journal*. Findings from the National Assessment of Educational Progress can guide high schools in determining what understanding should represent.[8]

The College Board's contribution to making high school studies more meaningful bears mention here, especially in connection with three of its programs. The Advanced Placement Program annually reaches 400,000 students attending half the nation's 21,000 high schools, offering them college-level studies. Another College Board program, Equity 2000, being piloted at six sites, aims to raise achievement and aspirations by enrolling all students in algebra and geometry. This program, designed particularly with minority students in mind, is underpinned by ongoing professional development, closer ties between school and home, academic enrichment activities, links with colleges, and careful monitoring of results. Finally, the College Board's Pacesetter Program applies the principles of the reform movement to create six entirely new courses for high school students with three of the courses—mathematics, English, and science—functioning as capstone courses that pull together and build on what students learned earlier in those subjects.

In calling on the "high school community" to define graduation standards we mean to underscore the need to enlist an assortment of local people in what should be a grassroots effort. High school graduates ought to be the beneficiaries of the contributions of the many people around them who end up sharing a stake in the students' success. We hope that the process produces wide backing for the goals of the high school and that members of the community will then contribute to helping students achieve success. It falls to each constituency to play a role in the realization of the goals. Students themselves have vast responsibilities under this approach. They should apply themselves to their studies and take advantage of the learning opportunities afforded them. We envision reciprocal responsibilities for each segment of the community. Broadly, the accountability of each constituency might work as follows:

Teachers should use their professional expertise to provide learning experiences that help students meet expected standards. Parents should act as advocates for their children and reinforce the efforts of the school in ways that make their offspring receptive to learning. The high school's administrators should provide vision, leadership, and advocacy. They should monitor instruction and learning and create a supportive environment for teachers and students who are trying to comply with the articulated goals. Community members and those representing local organizations should become knowledgeable about programs that foster student achievement and help the school gain financial support. They also must willingly serve as volunteers for mentoring programs and assist in the instructional program.

School board members should engage the community in a process to establish a vision, goals, and policies for the high school and strive to ensure that needed resources are provided. Board members should guarantee that budgetary priorities under the jurisdiction of the central office are in accord with academic goals of the high schools. The school district office should support and facilitate activities that enhance teaching and learning and create an environment that encourages educators in the high school to take the risks necessary to improve student achievement.

2. The high school will integrate its curriculum to the extent possible and emphasize depth over breadth of coverage.

Teaching subjects in isolation from each other, as high schools are wont to do, distorts knowledge (see "Organization and Time"). Teachers should expose students to the connections among and between subjects that high schools expect them to learn. On the most obvious level, science and mathematics fit together. So do English and social studies. Integration within a subject

may prove as valuable as integration across subjects. Teachers can present algebra and geometry, for instance, or biology, chemistry, and physics in integrated courses. When they seek natural points of connection for purposes of integration, teachers should not find it necessary to force integration of material. We are pleased that the Forum on Standards and Learning, a group made up of the College Board and six of the country's subject-matter associations will explore the ways in which new academic standards cut across subject areas. The group has begun work to identify how competencies that students learn in one subject apply to other subjects.

An illustration in just one state of what can be done to promote academic coherence can be found in Montana, where the National Science Foundation's Statewide Systemic Initiatives Program has supported the development of a mathematics curriculum that uses an integrated, interdisciplinary approach to integrate topics from the various areas of mathematics and to inject content from the arts, sciences, and technology. Professors from each of Montana's two public universities have worked with high school teachers to create a curriculum now used in a quarter of the state's ninth grades and which, eventually, will reach through the entire length of high school.[9]

Curriculum units constructed around themes or directed at answering fundamental questions or aimed at generative issues readily lend themselves to integrative education. This approach, used more frequently in elementary schools, tends to disappear in secondary education because of the emphasis on keeping the disciplines separate. The contents of a new magazine for teachers, *NEXUS*, illustrate what we have in mind. The premiere issue devoted itself to the play *The Lion in Winter*, a fictionalized account of a struggle for royal succession in 12th century England.[10] Essays in the issue examined feudalism, the Crusades, falconry, Gregorian chant, reliquary art, the physics of the crossbow, and the Arabic scientific and cultural influence on medieval Europe, providing any creative teacher with a cornucopia of ideas from which to draw lessons that cross the lines that usually separate subjects.

When Ernest L. Boyer wrote the book *High School* as a report for the Carnegie Foundation for the Advancement of Teaching, he called for "a new interdisciplinary vision" so that the content of the core curriculum would extend beyond the specialties to touch larger, more transcendent issues.[11] That was in 1983; the vision still has not taken hold, the coherence that it represents remaining an elusive goal for high schools. We realize that high schools need support for these kinds of changes and that teachers require assistance to identify points of connection among subjects. States and school systems, in turn, should make regulations more flexible to accommodate the possibility, for instance, that a student may meet a math requirement within what might be labeled a science course. Some institutions of higher education have forged ahead of high schools in this respect, as illustrated by innovations in the engineering program of Drexel University in Philadelphia that have blurred lines between the disciplines in freshman courses. Chemistry professors lead discussions on how to write research papers and humanities professors use scientific papers as a foundation for classes on the ethics of engineering.[12]

Teachers should regard curriculum as more than some inert substance lying on the pages of textbooks, waiting to be absorbed by students.

An emphasis on integration in high school teaching does not imply that teachers must achieve the impossible and master every subject. Teachers, however, should more readily venture beyond the boundaries of their own disciplines to grow familiar and comfortable with the neighboring intellectual terrain. Much of what occurs in multidisciplinary and interdisciplinary studies depends on teachers working in teams, each bringing his or her own special knowledge to the topic. Collaboration at its best enables teachers to fit together their individual contributions like pieces in an intricate jigsaw puzzle, each teacher handling portions of the curriculum appropriate to his or her expertise. Cooperative teaching of this sort must happen ever more frequently in high schools for the sake of studies that range across the subjects. This approach approximates what occurs in medical schools that take an organ system–based approach to the teaching of the basic sciences. Students, for instance, focus on

the circulatory system and professors—coordinating their lessons with each other—teach pharmacology, physiology, pathology, and other specialties within this unifying thematic framework.

The currently dominant subject-oriented approach to the curriculum leads to an obsessive desire to cram in as much about each subject as possible. Students end up skimming across the surface of a vast curriculum, leaving insufficient time to gain deep, significant understanding. They barely get wet as they swim hurriedly through an ocean of material. "The greatest enemy of understanding is coverage," write Howard Gardner and Veronica Boix-Mansilla, summing up one of the early findings of their research on teaching for understanding.[13] We prefer that high schools more tightly focus their curriculums and create learning situations in which students delve in depth into their assignments to attain understanding and mastery of the material. Students should take such an approach even if this means exposure to a less broad curriculum. States and school systems should reevaluate their requirements for breadth of coverage with an eye toward letting students cover less while expecting them to learn what they study more thoroughly.

3. Teachers will design work for students that is of high enough quality to engage them, cause them to persist, and, when successfully completed, result in their satisfaction and their acquisition of learnings, skills, and abilities valued by society.

Teachers should regard curriculum as more than some inert substance lying on the pages of textbooks, waiting to be absorbed by students. Upon the teachers in all high schools falls the responsibility for ensuring that the work that confronts students has the potential to engage them. Even difficult work need not be boring and inaccessible. Moreover, the level of engagement must be sufficient to command the continued interest of students despite their possible inability to grasp it immediately. This places on teachers the onus for designing lessons that are compelling in the face of difficulties since much that is worth learning calls for persistence and a sense of delayed gratification.

In part, this will occur more readily when students know that they face no penalty for trying and failing, that what is expected of them is merely that they keep trying.

We believe that part of the secret for successful teachers is to present students with work that causes them to think, reason, and use their minds well. It also helps if people other than the teacher—classmates, parents, other teachers—inspect the product of the students' efforts and affirm to the students the merit and worth of the work. Insofar as possible, students should have a choice of the types of assignments they do, understanding that specified learning is the objective and that standards will not be compromised or diluted. Presumably, the ability to choose will help sustain the high interest of the student.

We are talking here about creative teachers who use the curriculum to make their students perform as learners. In turn, this takes a great deal of effort on the part of the teacher. The very formidability of this task underlies our call throughout this report for preservice and inservice education of teachers that will equip them for the challenges of school improvement. Teachers should have the ability to develop activities for students that—while embodying the learning objectives—are clearly linked to intellectual products that the students value. When possible, students should take an active role in their learning rather than act as passive recipients of information passed on by textbooks and by teachers who do little more than lecture. The student, for instance, may keep a lab book, develop several examples for solving various equations, write a one-act play, or present an oral analysis of several interpretations of a historic event. This kind of an approach to the curriculum should be designed to cause students to find satisfaction in what they learn and to ensure parents and the larger public that, indeed, something worthwhile is occurring in the high school.

4. The content of the curriculum, where practical, will connect itself to real-life applications of knowledge and skills to help students link their education to the future.

High schools must put more emphasis on teaching students to apply what they learn. Too often, young people do not recognize connections between events in their everyday lives and what schools teach them; they cannot see the links between what they already know and what they are being taught. Part of teaching a subject well should be understood to include imparting the ability to use knowledge and to tie it to prior learning. This requires that high schools do more to present the curriculum in the context of

experiences that call upon students to apply knowledge in situations approximating those in which they will use knowledge in real life—"authentic learning," if you will.

Teachers should have the ability to develop activities for students that—while embodying the learning objectives—are clearly linked to intellectual products that the students value.

When we call for studies to connect "to real-life applications," critics may dismiss this recommendation as just one more plea for "relevance." We are not about to insist, however, that material has a legitimate place in the curriculum only if it connects immediately to the day-to-day lives of students. We believe that a high school need not apologize for teaching about, say, Sparta's role in the Peloponnesian Wars or the writings of Geoffrey Chaucer or how Joseph Priestley came to discover oxygen. On the other hand, whether or not they tie learning directly to real-life applications, teachers must make studies stimulating and challenging. If teachers can establish links to the lives of young people naturally and contextually, why not heighten the interest of the students and motivate them by explaining the importance that the material holds for them? "Higher order thinking skills and creativity are elicited when students have opportunities to work on projects that are at a level of complexity and duration that is comparable to real-world issues and problems," the American Psychological Association's Task Force on Psychology in Education said of what it called "motivation-enhancing learning tasks."[14]

Showing students how to apply what they know underscores the practicality of knowledge and heightens students' interest in the material. Much of what we learn does, in fact, have a connection to the world around us and teachers should make students aware of that fact. We do not mean to suggest that utilitarianism ought to dictate the curriculum. To the contrary, teachers must diligently invest some of their time in the direct teaching of abstract principles and basic concepts as a necessary prelude to the application of knowledge.[15] Ultimately, though, students should prepare themselves to use what they know. The application of knowledge enables people to earn a living or enjoy leisure or carry out daily tasks. Sometimes these applications are mundane, as in reading a bus schedule or balancing a checkbook, but more profound applications call upon someone, say, to learn from history or design a mathematical model.

> Once a high school decides what it wants to teach, evidence of whether or not students learned the material should rest on assessments based on what the school intended to teach.

The U.S. Labor Department's report by the Secretary's Commission on Achieving Necessary Skills (SCANS) calls for high school students to acquire "a new set of competencies and foundation skills."[16] Employers make no secret of what workers need in various fields and high schools have a defined role to play in moving young people toward the acquisition of these competencies and skills. The five areas of competency recommended by SCANS revolve around the use of resources, working with others, acquiring and using information, understanding complex interrelationships, and working with a variety of technologies. The three-part foundation for these competencies involves the teaching of basic skills in reading, writing, arithmetic, and listening and speaking; the cultivation of thinking skills; and the enhancement of personal qualities of responsibility, self-esteem, sociability, self-management, and integrity.

If, for instance, a teenager hopes eventually to be a dietary manager, a job that presumably requires education beyond high school, the student can acquire a foundation in high school for the knowledge and abilities that he or she will need. A job analysis of dozens of fields by the SCANS staff determined that, above all, a competent dietary manager must interpret and communicate infor-

mation, exercise leadership, understand systems, and serve clients and customers. Listening skills, honesty, and responsibility were judged the most important foundation skills for the job. While a student will not learn all the details of a dietary manager's work until sometime beyond high school, the student's preparation can start before getting a diploma.

Any young person persistent enough to stay the course should enjoy a sense of assurance about the future and derive the ability to apply what he or she has learned. Almost half the students who are graduated from American high schools do not go on to college and without adequate job preparation they face a bleak future. Even students preparing for college should have the chance to link their education to career paths or to special occupational interests. Seven states are moving toward certifying the job readiness skills of high school students, using variations of a model proposed by the National Center on Education and the Economy.[17] The federal government's School-to-Work Opportunities Act takes cognizance of these needs by providing funds for programs that try to address the transition to employment. An instrument that high schools might consider using to help students link their learning to occupational and career paths is Work Keys, an array of assessments offered since 1992 by American College Testing. These assessments determine the current skills of individuals, relate those skills to requirements that have been identified for certain jobs, and indicate what further instructional support the person needs to prepare for a particular job.

Educational institutions today pay lip service to the notion of lifelong education. High schools must give this concept credibility by encouraging a mindset in students that predisposes them toward continual reassessment and growth so that they can apply knowledge to the changing circumstances of their lives. They must learn to remain open to new ideas and to teach themselves outside formal education. Those prepared for lifelong learning can assess their own learning needs and manipulate the levers of knowledge so as to gain access to what they do not already know. A proper grounding in high school enhances and facilitates this process by underpinning it with a solid base of knowledge and with the skills by which to erect an intellectual structure that a person can continually renovate for the remainder of his or her life.

5. *Assessment of student learning will align itself with the curriculum so that students' progress is measured by what is taught.*

In recent years, the development and use of new kinds of assessment has been one of the pillars supporting the movement to restructure schools. Yet, one of the attendant difficulties has been a tendency for changes in assessment to go forward without commensurate concern for the related curriculum and pedagogy. "Simply administering tests without establishing links between and among the assessments and teacher development or instructional strategies is too superficial a change to have a discernible impact on schools," according to Richard J. Stiggins, founder and director of the Assessment Training Institute in Portland, Oreg., who criticizes the "school culture" for separating assessment from instruction.[18] Once a high school decides what it wants to teach, evidence of whether or not students learned the material should rest on assessments based on what the school intended to teach. In other words, a school should generally teach the material on which it will test students and test students on the material that was taught. This ostensibly obvious proposition, believe it or not, still does not necessarily prevail in classrooms around the country.

Too often, the content of examinations does not align itself with the actual curriculum and, while an examination may reveal what a student does not know, the lack of knowledge may be the result of the material never actually having been taught. A school, for instance, should reasonably expect a student who has been taught specific elements of good writing to display those elements in his or her writing. A student who has studied the properties of certain elements under laboratory conditions should be able to describe those properties and conduct equivalent experiments. A student who has learned certain axioms should provide a cogent explanation for solving geometric problems whose solutions depend on the application of those axioms. Alignment between curriculum and assessment is crucial, and without it, assessment may not offer a valid measurement of a student's progress.

6. *Each student will have a Personal Plan for Progress to ensure that the high school takes individual needs into consideration and to allow students, within reasonable parameters, to design their own methods for learning in an effort to meet high standards.*

More must happen in high schools to guarantee that students derive as much benefit as possible from the curriculum. This means planning and monitoring their academic experiences closely, course by course. Only disabled students can currently be certain of getting individual attention for their learning needs; federal law requires this kind of assistance for them. But the system should not compel a student to wear a label in order to gain notice. The creation of a Personal Plan for Progress will bring the needs of each student into sharper focus. The duties of the Personal Adult Advocate (see "School Environment") will include helping to develop a progress plan for each advisee. Advocates conferring with students on the plans must have time in their schedules to enable them to do the job properly.

> More must happen in high schools to guarantee that students derive as much benefit as possible from the curriculum. This means planning and monitoring their academic experiences closely, course by course.

Like the federally-mandated Individualized Education Plan for disabled students on which it is modeled, the progress plan will set learning goals for the student that are continually reevaluated. The plan will serve as a vehicle by which to gauge a student's progress toward meeting the learning standards embraced by the high school. The school will adjust the Personal Plan for Progress as dictated by the student's work (see "Assessment and Accountability"). In effect, a high school's educational goals and the proposed educational outcomes will shape the document and determine the changes made in it. The progress plan will be the vehicle by which a student can arrange for credit-bearing learning experiences beyond those that are part of the usual curriculum. For example, a student who wants to study a foreign language not available at the high school might designate a nearby community college as the site for such work. Or a student who wants to study the role of, say, jazz in the Harlem of the 1920s might specify the broad details of an independent project.

By the time a student reaches the halfway point in high school, the Personal Plan for Progress should start emphasizing a transition plan to direct the student's curricular goals toward whatever it is that the young person wants to do after earning a diploma. Even a dropout will have a progress plan so that the youngster leaves with a blueprint for making as good use as possible of the immediate future and perhaps for returning to formal education. As part of their progress plans, students will assemble reports of achievement that they could review with parents and, later, submit to colleges and potential employers. The information in this report would go well beyond the traditional transcript; the school might eventually place it on a CD-ROM so that a job interviewer or a college admissions officer could review samples of actual work done by the student. The report of achievement might borrow from the Record of Achievement that high school students in Great Britain maintain. This cumulative record of a British student's progress is kept in a ring-binder that grows thicker with time. It includes letters from adults who supervised the student in out-of-school internships or in community service. A student who does not continue on to college can take the Record of Achievement to a job interview.

7. The high school will promote cocurricular activities as integral to an education, providing opportunities for all students that support and extend academic learning.

The concept of "extracurricular" serves no useful purpose. Anything extra occupies a position peripheral to the school's main mission. We propose to scrap this outmoded term and instead call these activities "cocurricular," emphasizing that they are integral to the educational program. The very act of reexamining school activities and designating those that are bona fide as cocurricular implies that such pursuits—whether or not they carry academic credit—have legitimate links to regular courses and to the purposes of the high school. A high school properly provides for social and personal needs, as well as for those that are strictly academic. Given the benefits that students can obtain, high schools should promote cocurricular activities for all students. Cocurricular pursuits, after all, can undergird the goal of teaching students

to be responsible and fulfilled human beings, providing them with opportunities that develop character, critical thinking, sociability, and specific skills.

For these reasons, educators should evaluate cocurricular activities—including sports, the single largest area of participation—in terms of the support they provide for the school's broader objectives. It is not unreasonable, in order to justify school-sponsored activities, to hold professional educators responsible for making sure that connections to learning exist. An athletic coach who endorses a win-at-any-cost philosophy, for instance, has no business overseeing a cocurricular activity in a high school. Essentially, all activities carried out under the aegis of a high school should be viewed in terms of their potential contribution to the school's overall goals for young people. This imperative applies to athletics and clubs as much as it does to student government and publications. A high school should seek to engage as many students as possible in cocurricular activities, following a philosophy that students will miss a valuable part of their education if they do not participate. The cocurricular program, therefore, should offer sufficient variety to appeal to a wide range of student interests.

The concept of "extracurricular" serves no useful purpose. … We propose to scrap this outmoded term and instead call these activities "cocurricular," emphasizing that they are integral to the educational program.

Those connected with the activities, both students and their adult sponsors, must understand how each activity fulfills the larger purposes of the high school. Evidence from a U.S. Department of Education study shows that participants in cocurricular activities have more consistent attendance, better academic achievement, and higher aspirations than non-participants.[19] In addition, another study shows that students who devote 5 to 19 hours a week to cocurricular pursuits are less likely to use drugs or drop out of school, though athletes were more apt than non-athletes to engage in binge drinking.[20] Cocurricular programs should generally yield to academic courses, however, when conflicts of time arise. We hope that schools will reduce the potential for such conflicts by creating flexible schedules (see "Organization and Time").

8. A high school will reach out to the elementary and middle level schools from which it draws students to help those schools understand what kind of foundation students need for success in high school and to respond to the needs of the lower schools for policies at the high school that reinforce earlier education.

articulation

Just as higher education should respond to pre-collegiate education, high schools must be sensitive to the needs and concerns of elementary and middle level schools. The progression of students along an educational continuum proceeds most effectively when the various levels mesh. Success in high school depends very much on the work that a student does in the earlier grades. Pre-collegiate education, from pre-kindergarten through high school, should cohere as an experience in which the curriculum fits together to form a reasoned whole. Yet, high schools tend to ignore the so-called feeder schools, arrogantly assuming that articulation will take care of itself. Unfortunately, all too many students enter high school without the academic preparation to cope with the curriculum. These students either flounder in regular courses or get shunted into courses with meager content.

High schools can help avert such misfortunes by establishing liaisons with middle level schools—and with elementary schools, too—to make students and teachers in those schools better aware of the expectations to come. Efforts to strengthen relationships should include the tutoring of younger children by high school students and faculty-to-faculty programs. High schools must reach out to parents, too, while their children are still in the lower schools. High schools should also adjust their programs to take into consideration the reforms that occur in earlier grades. Notable in this regard is the failure of so many high schools to institute structural and curricular changes that align their programs with the innovations offered to students by middle level schools that have incorporated the restructuring provisions of the report *Turning Points*.[21]

A final facet of this accent on articulation involves the connections that high schools form with each other. High schools within the same district have a ready basis for affinity. In school systems with a single high school, links should be formed with high schools in neighboring districts, as well as with nearby nonpublic high schools. Such bonding could promote cooperative ventures that either save money or embellish the curriculum by creating critical mass where a single high school could not undertake a venture on its own. Faculty members, too, can benefit from associations with colleagues at other high schools, especially when few teachers in their own high school share their special interests. ■

Responsibility for implementing instructional strategies ultimately rests in the hands of individual teachers who should prepare themselves well and be able to utilize a variety of strategies, in addition to lecturing, for effective student learning. The principal will lead a constant search for better instruction, setting standards for acceptable teaching practices and providing support, resources, and ongoing professional development to facilitate effective instructional strategies.

chapter two
INSTRUCTIONAL STRATEGIES
Engaging Students in Their Own Learning

1. Each high school teacher will have a broad base of academic knowledge with depth in at least one subject area.

2. Teachers will know and be able to use a variety of strategies and settings that identify and accommodate individual learning styles and engage students.

3. Teachers will be adept at acting as coaches and as facilitators of learning to promote more active involvement of students in their own learning.

4. Teachers will teach in ways that help students to develop into competent problem solvers and critical thinkers.

5. Teachers will convey a sense of caring to their students so that their students feel that their teachers share a stake in their learning.

6. Teachers will utilize technology in their instruction in ways that improve student learning.

7. Teachers will integrate assessment into instruction so that assessment does not merely measure students, but becomes part of the learning process itself.

priorities for renewal

1. Each high school teacher will have a broad base of academic knowledge with depth in at least one subject area.

We want to signal our desire that the best and the brightest be eager and willing to join the faculties of high schools. Along with preparation for teaching at least one subject in depth, those who study for work in high school classrooms should take a full complement of liberal arts courses in the company of majors in those disciplines. We envision the ideal high school teacher as one with a breadth of knowledge. The best teachers transmit the joy of learning to their students, over and over again. It is not only that teachers steeped in knowledge have more to give their students, but that the confidence that comes with authority over subject matter enriches their teaching. Beyond this, a teacher must hone his or her communications abilities, serving as a model for the kinds of writing, speaking, and listening skills that he or she wants to cultivate in students.

Someone teaching at the high school level should possess a firm grasp of the foundational underpinnings and the associated ethical implications in at least one subject area. Such expertise requires more than having studied a collection of introductory courses in a college major. We want to emphasize in connection with this recommendation and one that we will make later in the report to reorganize academic departments (see "Organization and Time") that we unequivocally applaud the kind of specialization that produces experts in the individual subject areas. Students deserve no less in their teachers. In fact, we see it as the responsibility of teachers to keep up-to-date in changes in the disciplines and to remain active in the professional disciplinary associations. There is no contradiction between this goal and that of encouraging teachers to teach in ways that cause students to approach knowledge from a multidisciplinary perspective. A teacher should pursue specialization in a spirit that inclines him or her to use the advantage of disciplinary strength to make connections across subjects.

2. Teachers will know and be able to use a variety of strategies and settings that identify and accommodate individual learning styles and engage students.

A problem plaguing high schools has been that too many teachers teach in only one way, that is by the lecture method—the same way they were taught. They often feel that lecturing is the most expeditious method for covering a large volume of material. Students unable to comprehend the material from that single perspective are frequently offered no alternative. They encounter lecture after lecture as their teachers predictably resort to this lone mode of instruction, broken only by brief exchanges of questions and answers that hardly amount to true discourse. Too often, this approach leaves students unengaged, not caught up in the lesson, which is centered more on the teacher than on the student. Even students who repeat a course in high school usually are fed an identical dosage of the medicine that they could not digest in the first place.

Lecturing will always have a place in teaching and, indeed, some material is dealt with most appropriately in a lecture. A well-delivered lecture can encapsulate a world of knowledge and stimulate a listener to scale new intellectual heights. But lecturing must cease to be the sole way of teaching. Teachers should prepare themselves to offer courses that take advantage of methods that depend less on the teacher as purveyor of all wisdom. Students learn differently from one another and teachers should use a variety of instructional methods to reach everyone in the classroom, a change that will exact some investment on the part of school systems and teachers. As Larry Cuban points out, schools that want teachers to shift their instructional emphasis must realize that the change will require more of the time and energy of teachers and that they will need help "to put complex ideas into practice."[22] The ability of teachers to employ appropriate strategies will be enhanced by an understanding of cognitive development and findings from brain research that ought to be part of their ongoing education, especially as they strive to design lessons for individual learners.

Student-centered approaches that take advantage of research findings on learning involve youngsters more directly in their own education, tending to make the content of lessons more memorable. Seminars, cooperative learning, debates, field experiences, independent study, and laboratories all possess this potential. The lesson can captivate the youngster when a teacher finds an approach that strikes a responsive chord. Researchers have demonstrated that levels of engagement increase and academic achievement rises in schools that use these various restructuring practices.[23] Furthermore, the results of a survey by Public Agenda contain evidence that people approve of measures to engage students in their learning. This nonprofit public opinion research and education organization found that 86 percent of Americans think that "schools should place much greater emphasis on making learning enjoyable and interesting to high school students."[24]

Surely, teachers can find ways to encourage students—acting alone or in groups—to take initiative in acquiring knowledge. The teacher may, for instance, list key questions to guide this inquiry or provide students with the titles of books and articles that are pertinent to uncovering the knowledge. But upon the student falls the responsibility for unlocking the knowledge, analyzing it, synthesizing it, and presenting it as a body of material over which he or she has taken possession. This cannot happen all the time, but when it occurs the student, in effect, "constructs" knowledge. This way of learning leaves a deeper impression on a student than merely being told what he or she should know. In student-centered instruction, the student, not the teacher, becomes the "maker" of knowledge. Students discover on their own what teachers under most circumstances are accustomed to "revealing" to students. A skilled teacher diagnoses the needs of individual students, prescribes appropriate learning strategies for each based on the student's knowledge and skills, and evaluates the results with an eye toward adjusting his or her instructional methods. This approach takes more time and usually less material gets covered, but less will be more when students thoroughly understand what they have studied and absorb it into their permanent base of knowledge.

3. Teachers will be adept at acting as coaches and as facilitators of learning *to promote more active involvement of students in their own learning.*

Imagine what would happen if teachers in all courses acted more like the ablest athletic coaches. No coach shoots a basket or swings a bat for a youngster. A coach instructs in an active and involved way that leads to actual performance by the student. Precedent for this approach exists in some academic areas. Good teachers of drama and of writing, for example, are essentially coaches who perform their jobs in this manner. Why not also have science coaches and mathematics coaches and history coaches and literature coaches? They could work

in ways that motivate students to take more responsibility for their learning. The teacher, as facilitator, can guide the student through the thickets of knowledge, pointing out the pitfalls and providing tips to avoid entanglement in the underbrush while the student actually blazes the trail.

No coach shoots a basket or swings a bat for a youngster. A coach instructs in an active and involved way that leads to actual performance by the student.

Coaching involves a kind of teaching that creates active learners. The student investigates multiple approaches to solving a math problem or expounds on the meaning of the novel or conducts the physics experiment. But the teacher-coach remains nearby—observing, asking questions, prodding the student to reflect on the product of his or her efforts. The student's response or performance—the learning experience—becomes the subject of the coaching. What we have here, according to Theodore R. Sizer, founder of the Coalition of Essential Schools, is a student's "gaining skill through critiqued experience."[25] Good teachers have always infused their teaching with coaching. A successful tutorial session casts the teacher as coach. The Socratic method is as old as, well, Socrates. A teacher who turns a student's question back on the student and requests clarifications, all the while providing information for the student to ponder, provokes the student to discover his or her own answer, pushing the student to the limits of his or her knowledge.

John I. Goodlad's studies point to the potential benefits available when students take greater responsibility for their own learning. He found that only 76 percent of the time in a typical high school classroom was devoted to "instruction." Most of the remainder was spent on such routines as taking attendance, passing out papers, and giving instructions to students. Even during the three-quarters of the time given over to instruction, however, there was a "low incidence of activities involving active modes of learning."[26] If teachers conducted their classes so that they more often acted as coaches and students pursued more of their learning on their own, then many of the youngsters would be able to continue learning during the time now consumed by routines and even the learning itself might be more fruitful.

4. Teachers will teach in ways that help students to develop into competent problem solvers and critical thinkers.

Critical thinking and problem solving are areas in which the National Assessment of Educational Progress shows consistently that high school students fall short.[27] A high school education in America must equip students with the ability to draw inferences, make informed judgments, engage in logical reasoning, and solve problems. Students need to develop a mindset that orients them toward analyzing material and reaching conclusions about it. This happens too infrequently in America's high schools. Often, teachers let the acquisition of facts and

> **In student-centered instruction, the student, not the teacher, becomes the "maker" of knowledge. Students discover on their own what teachers under most circumstances are accustomed to "revealing" to students.**

basic skills become the end product of instruction, depriving youngsters of an education rich in nuances and deeper meanings. We do not want to disparage the learning of facts; a good knowledge base serves as a foundation for growth. We prefer, though, to emphasize the acquisition and application of facts through thinking and problem solving. It is worth noting, incidentally, that a student need not commit a knowledge base entirely to memory in this technological era if he or she gains the ability to identify what information is needed and learns how to obtain that information at the flick of a finger.

Pedagogy must orient itself toward higher order thinking skills, whatever the subject matter of the lesson.

Students learn how to reason and solve problems when teachers embed problems in the curriculum. Students evolve into critical thinkers when teachers challenge them to burrow into material so as to analyze and judge it. We are impressed by the five "Habits of the Mind" that Central Park East Secondary School in New York City cultivates in its courses:

- Weighing evidence—How credible is the evidence for what we think we know?

- Awareness of varying viewpoints—Whose viewpoint is this and what other viewpoints might there be?

- Seeing connections and relationships—How are things connected and what is here that we have seen before?

- Speculating on possibilities—Can we imagine alternatives?

- Assessing value both socially and personally—What difference does it make and who cares?[28]

5. Teachers will convey a sense of caring to their students so that their students feel that their teachers share a stake in their learning.

Students tell us that it makes a difference to have a teacher who they believe cares about them. Critics of high schools may regard the feelings of students as relatively low on the order of priorities. Yet, from the perspective of young people, whose confidence often is shaky and whose motivation is problematic, the attitude of the teacher looms large, affecting the very outcome of the lesson. Youngsters may not try as hard in the face of what they consider the teacher's indifference. When children struggle in school, parents frequently hear the words: "The teacher doesn't like me." This perception, whether or not well-founded, can demoralize students. Research in 24 elementary schools across the country demonstrates, on the other hand, that when students experience caring at school they exhibit academic, social, and ethical benefits including greater enjoyment of class, stronger motivation to act kindly and helpfully toward others, and stronger feelings of social competence.[29]

We are not talking here about teachers being buddies of students. Rather, the issue revolves around the teacher's professionalism. A teacher must, above all, know the material and the pedagogy for presenting it. But if being expert in instructional strategies includes the ability to engage the learner—and we believe it does—then, as a corollary, good teachers are adept at establishing the kind of teacher-student relationship that will help make the child receptive to learning. Otherwise, the ground may lie fallow. Educational researchers have found that caring fosters the emotional and intellectual development of students and affects the receptivity of students to teaching.[30] In propounding a model for the elementary school of the future, Ernest L. Boyer said that one of the six characteristics of such an institution should be that it is "a caring place, where the principal, teachers, and students are respectfully attentive to each other."[31]

Assessment as a dynamic, evolving process can reveal at any point what has been learned and what remains to be learned, functioning as a blueprint for further learning.

The *Phi Delta Kappan,* in the lead article of its January 1995 issue, highlighted the idea that schools must fill a vacuum in the lives of many children by giving more emphasis to the "three C's of care, concern, and connection." This means having schools take on some of the attributes of a good home.[32] *The Kappan*—apparently persuaded of the importance of the topic—went on to devote its entire May 1995 issue to the theme of "Youth and Caring." We hope that those teachers who already display caring will serve as models to their colleagues. At the most basic level, all teachers should like kids and show enthusiasm for their learning. Young people sense the ambivalence and resentment of teachers and administrators who are frustrated, burned out, or just plain dissatisfied with their jobs. Such people should get out of education.

6. Teachers will utilize technology in their instruction in ways that improve student learning.

Teachers should use every tool in the kit to engage students and to facilitate their learning. The computer, the videodisc, the CD-ROM, virtual reality, and other technological devices can augment and even substitute for lectures and books. Students should have benefit of word processing and other forms of technology, which will

bring about changes in instructional methods and in ways of learning. In biology, for example, students can now study the anatomy of a frog in bloodless fashion, "dissecting" it via a three-dimensional computer program without having to lift a scalpel to the body of the actual animal. In mathematics, technology not only allows students to make connections between geometric and algebraic models, but it also lets them investigate problems and arrive at solutions that previously had to wait until they studied calculus.

The responsibility falls to teachers to learn how to incorporate technology into their teaching strategies. In planning a curriculum unit, the teacher should consider how to strengthen the lesson at each point of the way by employing technology. To do so is akin to what conscientious teachers have always done in, say, determining an appropriate bibliography for a particular curriculum unit. This means, too, that teachers ought to identify databases for students to use and inform students when electronic spreadsheets will make it easier for them to organize the material they are studying. In the same way, an appropriate CD-ROM used at the proper moment can inject immediacy into what might otherwise be just another dull lesson. Virtual reality can make a lesson particularly memorable. And dialing into the Internet may allow a student to reach sources whose firsthand knowledge of a situation can provide original source material.

7. Teachers will integrate assessment into instruction so that assessment does not merely measure students, but becomes part of the learning process itself.

Teachers should not separate assessment from instruction. An ongoing assessment process will enable teachers to monitor students' progress and adjust instruction continually. This sort of "formative" approach to assessment will help ensure that agreed-upon learning goals shape the instruction. Curriculum and assessment are opposite sides of the same coin and the assessment can, in effect, serve as the curriculum. This way a student can demonstrate his or her level of understanding even while learning the material. If, for example, a teacher wants to assess a student's understanding of the scientific method in conducting a particular physics experiment involving electromagnetic fields, the assessment can be the assignment itself. Let the student carry out the experiment until he or she demonstrates the desired competency and understanding. Assessment should be about learning, not about catching students in mistakes. In much the same way, assessment of a student's ability to write a paper about *Hamlet* should be an evolving process with the teacher marking and providing feedback on successive drafts—in effect, assessing the work—as the student hones the essay into a finished product.

Assessment should flow largely from the idea that it promotes learning. "Summative" assessments that come at the conclusion of the learning process and sum up the results will probably always have some role in education, but assessment serves teaching and learning best when teachers link it closely to the ongoing instructional process. Assessment as a dynamic, evolving process can reveal at any point what has been learned and what remains to be learned, functioning as a blueprint for further learning. A successful marriage between assessment and instruction depends on preparing teachers to walk down this particular aisle with the knowledge and confidence to make the union work, a fact emphasized by a federally sponsored study that reached this finding: "The professional support and training of teachers is emerging as the pivotal factor for determining the success of the assessment reform process."[33] ■

School environ-
ment should be a
catalyst for ensuring
that students pursue
their education under
circumstances that
foster the very
difficult work of
teaching and learn-
ing. This means that
the principal and
everyone else respon-
sible for the high
school must create a
climate favorable to
education, whether it
occurs inside or out-
side the main build-
ing, and do every-
thing possible to
sustain that climate.

chapter three
SCHOOL ENVIRONMENT
Creating a Climate Conducive to Teaching and Learning

1. The high school community, which cannot be value-neutral, will advocate and model a set of core values essential in a democratic and civil society.

2. Experiences in high school will acknowledge multiple talents and ways of learning to help students achieve the meaningful success that leads to further achievement.

3. Every high school student will have a Personal Adult Advocate to help him or her personalize the educational experience.

4. The school will accord meaningful roles in the decision-making process to students, parents, and members of the staff to promote an atmosphere of participation, responsibility, and ownership.

5. In order to maintain a positive environment, each high school will ensure that any student who brings a weapon into a high school, sells illegal drugs in the school, or behaves violently in the school will immediately forfeit the right to attend that particular school.

   Zero tolerance

6. Agreements that school systems negotiate with teachers, principals, and other personnel will be accompanied by a Student Impact Statement to help warrant that contracts and other agreements consider the best interests of students.

7. Every school system will ensure that facilities used by its high schools are clean, attractive, safe, and well equipped.

Core Values of the Bourne Public Schools.
- ✓ We value the pursuit of academic excellence
- ✓ We believe in a safe and nurturing environment
- ✓ We value respect and personal growth

priorities *for renewal*

1. The high school community, which cannot be value-neutral, will advocate and model a set of core values essential in a democratic and civil society.

America's high schools should reclaim the moral high ground from which to impart the values upon which the nation predicates its democratic and civil society. This means that schools must unabashedly teach students about such key virtues as honesty, dependability, trust, responsibility, tolerance, respect, and other commonly-held values important to Americans. Some educators may feel uncomfortable about accepting this assignment, but we believe certain enduring virtues are universal to principled Americans. In an era when children are killing children and children are giving birth to children, high schools cannot afford to shirk this duty.

Young people must learn the meaning of life in a democratic and civil society while attending high school. They must prepare to assume the obligations of citizenship. The role for high schools to play in this process starts with efforts to allow students to learn how to be responsible members of the school community itself. This effort will be reflected in the curriculum, not by any sort of brainwashing, but by making certain that—when appropriate—high schools infuse their studies with lessons that prod students to examine, weigh, and practice the core values of a democratic and civil society. Sometimes teachers may devote specific lessons to the teaching of values, but we prefer to see such instruction embedded in the regular curriculum and taught in the context of literature, social studies, science, and various courses.

Furthermore, values can be modeled in the conduct of members of the high school community and accentuated by the policies and practices under which that community functions. The Communitarian Network captured the essence of this idea in its platform document advocating that character-building should permeate every aspect of school life. It stated: "The way sports are conducted, grades are allotted, teachers behave, and corridors and parking lots are monitored all send moral messages and significantly affect character development."[34] In other words, the larger lessons that prepare students for civic life arise from experiences in school that lead them to value democratic and civil principles.

Those skeptical of attempts by public schools to imbue students with specific values maintain that such endeavors are widely opposed, but we believe otherwise. The Phi Delta Kappa/Gallup Poll revealed that 69 percent of Americans think it possible to agree on a set of basic values for schools to teach. More than 90 percent of the respondents concurred on the propriety of teaching students about honesty, democracy, acceptance of people of different races and backgrounds, patriotism, caring for friends and family members, moral courage, and treating others as you would like others to treat you.[35] The Aspen Declaration of Character Education, signed in 1992 by 30 educators, youth organization leaders, and ethicists, set forth eight principles for character education, stating that "core ethical values transcend cultural, religious, and socio-economic differences."[36]

> . . . schools must unabashedly teach students about such key virtues as honesty, dependability, trust, responsibility, tolerance, respect, and other commonly-held values important to Americans.

But high schools are not islands. They depend on the rest of society to reinforce the lessons of the classroom. Families and entire neighborhoods must accept responsibility for supporting the values that schools try to impart. Young people need to see people around them live by the standards that the school strives to instill in them. Society does not want to abandon this responsibility entirely to the schools, as attested to by data that show that Americans, more than people in other countries, believe that the home should take precedence over the school in the teaching of values.[37] Ideally, the home will serve as the main site for character formation and the high school will try to act in concert with the home. Parents and other adults must acknowledge, though, that unless they demonstrate that they cherish constructive values, the message of the school will be ambiguous to youngsters.

2. Experiences in high school will acknowledge multiple talents and ways of learning to help students achieve the meaningful success that leads to further achievement.

High schools should recognize the multiplicity of differences represented in any single classroom. Students differ in their talents and in their ways of learning, providing human variations that should be used as paving blocks on the road to success. These differences are natural and should not be viewed as rendering students more or less worthy than their classmates, a fact noted by the American Psychological Association's Task Force on Psychology in Education when it observed that "learners differ in their preferences for learning mode and strategies, and unique capabilities in particular areas."[38] Teachers should identify students' strengths and then structure teaching to appeal to those attributes, lending students the help they need to succeed. Students can learn to identify and cultivate areas of strength so that they gain appreciation for personal assets that are real and enduring.

Debates over whether schools should try to bolster the egos of their students sometimes degenerate into derisive comments about false pride of accomplishment. It is essential that young people build confidence on accurate appraisals that they make of themselves. False pride, like a castle of sand, washes away with the next tide. We agree that students' heads should not be inflated with hot air. But high schools have a genuine problem in dealing with young people who doubt their own abilities and react by withdrawing or becoming hostile to others. Such behavior undermines the learning community that should exist in each high school. High schools can, however, take steps to help students discover their strengths and encourage them to perform schoolwork that is worthy of praise. Awards for first-place finishers are fine, but schools should supplement them by recognizing students who, for example, show improvement or great effort.

Admittedly, the research points to only a moderate correlation between the opinions that young people have about themselves and how well they do academically. Good feelings about themselves apparently are not a cause of achievement, but a result of achievement. In other words, confidence based on past achievement can contribute to future academic achievement by adding to a student's faith in his or her ability to repeat past successes. While a high estimate of one's self may not produce academic achievement, the opposite condition—low self-confidence—can hinder progress by making students feel worthless and unmotivated.[39] Therefore, high schools should foster experiences that lead to genuine success for students, experiences upon which youngsters can build confidence. Other segments of society share this responsibility, too, but the high school has a special role because of the many learning situations that arise each day in which the outcome can be either success or failure.

3. Every high school student will have a Personal Adult Advocate to help him or her personalize the educational experience.

Each student needs to know that at least one adult in the school is closely concerned with his or her fate. The Personal Adult Advocate will be that person. The relationship between the student and the advocate should ensure that no youngster experiences the sense of isolation that frequently engulfs teenagers during this critical period of their lives. Having someone on his or her side can help a young person feel a part of the school community. Individual teachers, counselors, and other school personnel sometimes serve as buffers for students with whom they develop a special rapport. But this informal process does not usually vest in educators the kind of responsibility that we have in mind. The homeroom arrangement, for instance, was supposed to provide such support, but it has become perfunctory at most high schools. The Personal Adult Advocate will assume a function beyond that usually associated with a homeroom teacher or even a guidance counselor. Some high schools may create an advocate program by enhancing the role of homeroom teachers so that they can truly take on these duties. A student should ordinarily remain assigned to the same advocate throughout the high school years. We expect the advocate to meet regularly throughout the year on an individual basis with about 15–20 students.

Versions of this approach have been used in such places as New Trier High School in suburban Chicago, Shoreham-Wading River Middle School on Long Island, N.Y., Indian Creek High School in Trafalgar, Ind., and Freedom High School in Albuquerque, N.Mex. At Freedom High, for instance, the principal, the counselor, and the teachers each advise 20 students, finding time to confer individually with students at least once a week. High schools should restructure schedules (see "Organization and Time") to allow this to happen. Admittedly, this recommendation will add to the already-busy work day of teachers, but high schools can attempt to move in this direction incrementally. Virtually all the professionals in the school, including the principal, other administrators, and professional support personnel can serve as advocates for students. The advocate, among other things, will help to tailor a Personal Plan for Progress for each student (see "Curriculum"). This plan serves as a map that guides the student through high school and points the way toward unexplored territory beyond high school. Furthermore, an advocate will facilitate the student's dealings with others in the school—identifying problems that should be taken up with a guidance counselor, speaking with a teacher or student with whom the student is having difficulty, and, perhaps, visiting the student's home.

Teachers and other professionals who become Personal Adult Advocates will need assistance. Guidance counselors are best positioned to train the advocates and to coordinate the program, providing the ongoing support that makes it work. Advocates can perform many of the advising tasks, referring students to guidance counselors when they see the need. Guidance counselors should then be able to deal more closely with matters involving larger issues of academic achievement, a focus that they have not always maintained in the past. The College Board warns in a report on counselors that often in addressing developmental needs in a broad and comprehensive manner, they "do not clearly establish the primacy of student academic achievement in their goal statements and activities."[40] This approach will improve relationships between students and teachers, allowing guidance counselors the time to concentrate on the main learning issues that confound students.

4. The school will accord meaningful roles in the decision-making process to students, parents, and members of the staff to promote an atmosphere of participation, responsibility, and ownership.

People more readily commit themselves to an institution that accords them a measure of influence over its operations. Members of the high school community should have the opportunity to participate on panels, site-based councils, evaluation groups, and other bodies that shape policy. Each high school must decide how to allot decision-making power. We are not calling for an upheaval of authority, but rather for mechanisms to ensure input and participation by those most closely affected by the high school.

Teachers and other educators associated with the high school have ideas that can assist greatly in policy considerations. Empowering them to contribute to the decision-making process can lead them to be more dedicated and effective educators. Students who have a role in setting learning goals will feel a vested interest in meeting those goals. They need to realize that they hold some control over their own destiny.

Teachers should identify students' strengths and then structure teaching to appeal to those attributes, lending students the help they need to succeed.

We see merit in including students on various committees that determine policies that affect, say, discipline, grading standards, and participation on sports teams. A high school that follows such a philosophy will do all it can, for example, to foster a viable student government. It will also convene forums in which students can share ideas about school reform and equip students with mediation skills so that they can help resolve problems in the school. Young people learn how to exercise responsibility by having the chance to do so. Students should know that things do not "just happen" to them, that they can act to affect outcomes.

It is not sufficient, though, to take note only of teachers and students when trying to encourage a wider sense of ownership. Prospects for academic success—and that most concerns us here—grow when parents also feel a stake in the high school. A nationwide study based on the U.S. Department of Education's 1993 National Household Education Survey confirmed that parents exhibit less interest in their children's schooling with each passing year, leaving them far less involved by the time sons and daughters reach high school than they were when the same children were in elementary school. The same study found, however, that students whose parents stay involved tend to fare better academically and socially than others.[41]

Zero Tolerance

5. In order to maintain a positive environment, each high school will ensure that any student who brings a weapon into a high school, sells illegal drugs in the school, or behaves violently in the school will immediately forfeit the right to attend that particular school.

School climate acts as a sort of catalyst, not visible in educational outcomes, but very much affecting the process of teaching and learning that leads to those outcomes. Safety and order must prevail at all times. Only in such an environment may teaching and learning thrive. For starters, this means making high school a place where everyone feels secure and relaxed. Youngsters who are intimidated and fearful cannot be at ease; they cannot give education the single-minded attention needed for success. Nor can teachers teach with the required clarity of purpose if they are anxious and worried about their own safety and that of their students. Almost 1 of every 10 high school students says he or she is a victim of bullying, physical attack, or robbery at or near school during a typical year.[42] High schools should declare unequivocally that weapons, illegal drugs, alcohol, and violent acts have no place in an academic setting.

Youngsters who are intimidated and fearful cannot be at ease; they cannot give education the single-minded attention needed for success.

In regard to drugs and alcohol, this is more than a health issue, as important as that is. Drug and alcohol abuse undermine the ability of users to be productive students, poisoning the atmosphere for everyone in the school. The blight of drugs has exacted a deadly toll from young people and alcohol, too, alters the course of lives. Drinking among teenagers frequently serves as a prelude to vandalism and rowdiness. The negative impact that drinkers in college have on other students was documented by research on 140 campuses. The study found that heavy drinkers were disproportionately responsible for unwanted sexual advances, fighting, and interrupting the studying of other students.[43] We think that the impact is no less deleterious when high school students drink.

Weapons possession by young people is part of a cycle of escalation in which some students maintain that they have no choice but to arm themselves against others whom they believe to be armed. Juveniles accounted for 23 percent of all the weapons arrests in the United States in 1993.[44] Almost half the students in New York City who carried weapons to schools said they did so for protection.[45] Given this fact, school officials are clearly obligated to collaborate with public authorities to protect students going to and from school so as to remove excuses for bearing weapons. So long as weapons are brought into high schools it will be that much more likely that provocations will be met by the brandishing of a gun or a knife. No district should compel students to attend a high school that operates under such adverse circumstances. As it is, more than half the students in junior and senior high schools give their schools only a "fair" or "poor" rating in protecting them from crime on school grounds.[46] The Gun-Free Schools Act that Congress passed in 1994 should strengthen the hands of high schools in ridding their classrooms and corridors of weapons.

Students, teachers, and everyone else in the building must be confident that they inhabit a secure and law-abiding environment in which officials will meet threats to the peace with swift and firm action. We envision a policy of zero-tolerance for weapons, drugs, and violent acts. Students barred from the school for violating this code of conduct will receive opportunities to attend alternative schools or, possibly, be isolated in separate sections of their regular schools. The chance to return to their original settings will be possible only after these students demonstrate their worthiness in alternative settings. We realize that rules to enforce this ban must be carefully crafted, especially in regard to disabled students whose rights are protected by a congressional act.

6. Agreements that school systems negotiate with teachers, principals, and other personnel will be accompanied by a Student Impact Statement to help warrant that contracts and other agreements consider the best interests of students.

Negotiated agreements with employees that affect high schools should redound to the best interests of students. Collective bargaining provisions, for instance, undermine education if they operate to the detriment of youngsters. Thus, we propose that a Student Impact Statement be written in conjunction with new agreements. The Impact Statement could be prepared as a result of school board policy. The preparation of such a document will encourage those who engage in school negotiations—on both sides of the table—to anticipate the effects that agreements will have on students. If, for instance, a school gains the right to have certain provisions of a teachers' contract waived, the Student Impact Statement could spell out the possible benefits and shortcomings for the instructional program. Or, if preparation time is added or taken away from teachers' schedules, the statement could discuss how students might be positively or negatively affected.

The physical setting of a high school should nurture a student in much the same way that the clean, safe interior of a home makes the youngster feel comfortable and secure.

The Student Impact Statement should be an impartial document, dispassionately setting forth expectations of how negotiated agreements will affect students. The impact statement is intended as a purely informational document and should not take sides, limiting its concern to the welfare of students. Each district would decide the composition of the panel charged with preparing the statement, emphasizing the inclusion of parents, members of civic watchdog groups, college professors, and students, as well. We are not so naive as to believe that the prospect of a Student Impact Statement will eliminate the pursuit of self-interest by parties to negotiated agreements. But we do think that placing agreements under the public microscope of what's-best-for-kids just might cause negotiators to think twice about some of their demands, and alert the public to the implications of the pacts that govern school policies.

7. Every school system will ensure that <u>facilities</u> used by its high schools are clean, attractive, safe, and well equipped.

The condition of facilities can affect the climate for learning. All aspects of the high school's physical envi-

ronment have an impact on students and their inclination to achieve. The physical setting of a high school should nurture a student in much the same way that the clean, safe interior of a home makes the youngster feel comfortable and secure. The physical environment of a high school ought to lend a sense of affirming, supporting, tolerating, accepting, and caring. Americans must provide the kinds of school facilities that show students that society values them. In this connection, districts should ensure that facilities are accessible to the disabled, which, after all, is a legal requirement. Furthermore, schools must provide for the safety of all people who use the facilities, making certain, for instance, that fire alarms and sprinkler systems work and that the design of parking lots protects pedestrians.

A report from the federal government's General Accounting Office estimates that schools in the United States need $112 billion to upgrade or repair their facilities, noting that as many as one-third of all schools need extensive repairs or replacement.[47] These findings reflect the fact that one-third of the 110,000 schools in the country were built before World War II and only about 1 of 10 schools was constructed since 1980.[48] In a survey of teachers in the late 1980s, the Carnegie Foundation for the Advancement of Teaching discovered that heating was considered a problem by 54 percent; cleanliness, by 51 percent; and the general condition of the physical plant, by 46 percent.[49] A good building does not necessarily make a good school and, in fact, one sometimes finds marvelous schools housed in centuries-old structures in European countries. But the morale and motivation of those in the building can sag—and safety can be imperiled—when a school of any age suffers neglect.

Districts everywhere in the United States exacerbated the physical problems of schools in recent years by deferring maintenance in response to budgetary pressures. The District of Columbia Committee on Public Education, looking at the dismal state of school facilities in that city, said that the message to students was that "...what is going on inside is not important, that the school system is uncaring, and that neglect is tolerated. A building in poor repair contributes to the attitude and discipline problems among students, which in turn contribute to poor performance in schools."[50]

The physical condition of school buildings depends on

the attitudes and deportment of many people. As in a family, each member of the school community bears some responsibility for the well-being of the facilities. Japanese schools assign students to perform various maintenance tasks in their schools, leaving no doubt in the minds of young people about their role in the upkeep of their schools. Students in the United States should also come to understand, especially by the time they are teenagers, that they share an obligation to keep their schools in good condition. Litter and vandalism, for instance, do not miraculously appear as a result of infractions by evil elves. Responsibility for the upkeep of a high school extends more widely when the school opens its facilities to the neighborhood for various functions before and after classes, on weekends, and during vacations. Outsiders who use the school, like the students and the teachers, must respect the facilities and contribute toward keeping the building clean and in working order. ■

T

Technology is revolutionizing education and educators cannot afford to regard it as a frill or simply as an add-on. Careful planning should begin immediately in each high school to employ technology throughout the school and to integrate it into all aspects of the program. Boards of education must provide funds for the purchase of current technology and for enabling teachers to pursue ongoing education in technology.

chapter four
TECHNOLOGY
Making Way for Electronic Learning

1. School leaders will work with others to develop and implement a long-term strategic plan for use of technology in the school. The plan, including a code of ethics, will allow for ongoing changes in technology and adapt itself to continual changes in the school program.

2. Schools will make technology integral to curriculum, instruction, and assessment, accommodating different learning styles and helping teachers to individualize the learning process.

3. High schools will equip individual classrooms with the technology necessary to prepare students for life in the 21st century.

4. Budget allocations will be adequate to maintain current technology and to provide for ever-changing technology needs, including sufficient funds to permit access to all students and to use technology to deliver student services.

5. Technology will be a key part of both initial and continuing teacher education to provide teachers with the knowledge and skills they need to integrate technology into the curriculum and to adapt it to instructional strategies. To achieve these ends, school districts will hire teachers who can use technology to obtain information and who can incorporate technology into teaching and learning.

6. Every high school will designate a technology resource person to provide technical assistance and to consult with the staff to assist them in finding the people, information, and materials that they need to make best use of technology.

priorities for renewal

1. School leaders will work with others to develop and implement a long-term strategic plan for use of technology in the school. The plan, including a code of ethics, will allow for ongoing changes in technology and adapt itself to continual changes in the school program.

A high school fails to provide its teachers with a full range of instructional possibilities when it does not formulate a long-term plan for using technology, an omission that makes the educational program as incomplete as a bicycle with one wheel missing. Technology may well be the chalk of the 21st century. High school students readily recognize the significance of technology to their lives—even if their teachers do not—and come to school expecting to see technology integrated into their education. A high school that responds inadequately to this imperative is out of touch with its students and runs the risk of making their education appear irrelevant to them. This is an era, after all, when an entire book can be put on a microchip no larger than a fingernail and a student can summon up every word of the book instantly on a device small enough to nestle in one hand.

> High school students readily recognize the significance of technology to their lives—even if their teachers do not—and come to school expecting to see technology integrated into their education.

High schools can enrich and expand virtually every course in the curriculum when they employ computers and other technologies. A high school can multiply the data resources available to its students by linking its computers to create a local area network within the school and, going a step further, connect the school's computers to computers at other sites to give students access to what is known as a wide area network. Properly employed, technology will strengthen both the instructional and the administrative work of the school. A report by the North Central Regional Educational Laboratory argues that tech-nology is uniquely suited to promote school reform, citing the roles that technology can play in authentic and multidisciplinary tasks, performance-based assessment, interactive modes of instruction, heterogeneous grouping, collaborative work, student exploration, and teachers functioning as facilitators.[51]

The principal and other leaders in the school must step out front to help shape a technological vision, recognizing that any such plan never reaches completion because technology itself constantly evolves. Wise and productive use of technology in education requires careful preparation and periodic consultation with experts. Effective implementation of technology will precipitate changes in the school's policies, procedures, regulations, and staffing patterns—all of which should be anticipated in the planning. Schools should prepare for shifts in teaching and learning that will require continual revisions in how the school employs technology. All aspects of the school's use of technology, for whatever purpose, should be guided by a commitment to respect privacy and to uphold commonly accepted ethical standards. A school must be vigilant about monitoring adherence to these standards and should prepare a formal code of ethics to clarify the school's intentions.

2. Schools will make technology integral to curriculum, instruction, and assessment, accommodating different learning styles and helping teachers to individualize the learning process.

The use of technology in any high school begins with the proposition that technology is not an add-on to the program. Everyone must understand that full dedication to technology will be integral to the program, challenging traditional classroom structures and practices, transforming and forever altering curriculum, instruction, and assessment. Many high schools have already expanded access to library resources through technology, making electronic card catalogues, CD-ROMs, and databases available through the school's network of computers. Students at some such high schools also enjoy access to the data system in the evenings and on weekends by dialing into it from their home computers. Students with disabilities, among others, benefit from strategies and peripheral devices that use technology to permit them to carry out learning tasks that might otherwise be difficult if not impossible for them to do.

Technology, in effect, extends the curriculum, enabling students to pursue in-depth study more readily and giving them access to information that they could formerly obtain only with an expenditure of considerable time and effort. A curriculum can also employ technology to present material in ways that prod students to reflect on what they are learning and confront them with problems they must solve even if only through simulation. Some experts maintain that technology promises to produce particularly significant instructional breakthroughs in mathematics and science, two subjects that many high school students want as little to do with as possible. "When technology is effectively integrated into mathematics and science education, it can raise both the quality of teaching and the level of student understanding and achievement, just as it has made the high-performance workplace possible," says the Research and Policy Committee of the Committee for Economic Development.[52]

We recommend elsewhere in this report that instruction take on a more individualized aura (see "Curriculum"). Surely, technology will play a key role in achieving that objective. Students can become navigators of their own learning, steering themselves in the direction of more thorough learning simply by running their fingers across a keyboard or speaking to a voice-activated computer.

In addition to adapting technology to existing courses in ways that meet the individual needs of students, we hope that every high school will consider creating a course on technology itself. The goal of such a course would be not so much to make programmers of students or to explain the inner mechanics of computers, but to serve as a forum in which students can explore the best writings and ideas about technology itself. This way they can ponder the meanings of technology for the next century, the period in which they will spend the greatest portion of their lives.

Technology's influence on assessment will be no less profound than its impact on curriculum and instruction. In many ways, we are talking about the same thing since instruction and assessment should intertwine as the strands of a braid. The adaptations of technology for instruction ought to lead naturally to its use in assessment, whether the issue is writing a paper with a word processing program, working a mathematical problem on a cal-

culator, performing a chemistry experiment on the computer and analyzing the results on an electronic spreadsheet, poring over a computerized map in social studies to look at the shifting borders of the former Yugoslavia, or using a videodisc to study art. Furthermore, technology should make it easier to extend assessment beyond the work of individual students so that entire courses and even the school itself are more precisely evaluated.

3. High schools will equip individual classrooms with the technology necessary to prepare students for life in the 21st century.

At first, schools put all the computers in one room and sent students to that room so they could use them. Eventually, schools began installing some computers in some classrooms so that teachers might more readily incorporate technology into their lessons. Now, making a classroom ready for technology means providing equipment ranging from that which uses wires to that which uses no wires at all as, for example, the cellular phone. And, when wires are used, even what travels on the wires may vary. Fiber optics, for instance, uses light to carry electronic signals along bundled fibers of glass, each fiber smaller in diameter than a human hair, making it possible to transmit tens of thousands as much data as on a standard copper telephone line.

Some experts maintain that technology promises to produce particularly significant instructional breakthroughs in mathematics and science, two subjects that many high school students want as little to do with as possible.

Whether in the classroom or at home, high school students increasingly should have available the capacity to participate in what we now call distance learning. As the power of technology melts distances, students will be liberated from constraints of time and space. High schools must prepare for the fast-approaching day when their students pursue studies with teachers and professors they never meet face-to-face, instructors who work in schools and on campuses on which the students never set foot. Education thrives on information and high schools must prepare to exploit the ability to transmit data, text, graphics, and video.

In this regard, high schools should provide their students with access to the Internet and establish an acceptable code of ethics for its use. Congress could help with this goal by passing legislation proposed in 1995 to create a board that would advise the Federal Communications Commission on how schools could gain affordable access to the Internet. No more than an estimated 3 percent of the nation's classrooms now have access to the Internet.[53] We welcome the announcement by the AT&T Corporation that it will commit $150 million to help schools enhance their technology, including access to the Internet.

4. *Budget allocations will be adequate to maintain current technology and to provide for ever-changing technology needs, including sufficient funds to permit access to all students and to use technology to deliver student services.*

Allocations for technology should be as basic to the academic program as money spent for books. A high school needs adequate funds to fashion itself as a technology-rich environment, where thoughts about teaching and learning always incorporate considerations of calculators, computers, software, CD-ROMs, telecommunications, videodiscs, and other technologies that assist and promote learning. This means that the budget for technology cannot be a one-time item, abandoned after the original expenditures for hardware and software on the supposition that no more remains to be done. While certain outlays at the outset may satisfy start-up costs, the budget must continue to provide for maintenance, upgrading, added equipment, and retraining of staff.

During just the last decade, 20 generations of computers have come and gone. Therefore, schools must be wary of donations of computers that allow a tax deduction for the contributor and leave the school with a piece of outdated junk that does not synchronize with the rest of the school's computers. At the same time, schools should be fiscally responsible to the public in their pur-

chase and use of technology, relying on such guidelines as those based on a six-year study of the five Model Technology Schools that Florida established as a pilot project in 1988. Schools should exercise vigilance to ensure access to technology for all students, not just for a chosen few. Family income must not determine a student's degree of access to technology. To deny students equal opportunity of this sort is akin to distributing books to only a portion of the class. Every student attending high school today will live in a world in which technology will be ubiquitous.

media specialist + librarian

Funds spent on encyclopedias and other printed reference sources, for instance, should be reevaluated at a time when free or inexpensive electronic data can provide much the same information—and in a form that the school can inexpensively update. "Consider the *Encyclopaedia Britannica*," suggests Sarah Lyall, the former publishing correspondent for the *New York Times*. "The complete set costs more than $1,500, weighs 118 pounds, and takes up more than four feet of shelf space. A commensurate encyclopedia on CD-ROM—Microsoft's *Encarta*, for instance—costs $99.99, holds up to 650 megabytes of data, weighs under an ounce, and could fit in your purse."[54]

...the budget for technology cannot be a one-time item, abandoned after the original expenditures for hardware and software on the supposition that no more remains to be done.

Thus, creative planning can ease the fiscal strain when it comes to technology. Technology, for example, makes it unnecessary for a school to have multiple copies of the same reference work because databases on computers can provide multiple access so that dozens of students may consult the same page at once. Money-saving efforts might include a plan to use the technology facilities and databases of cooperating organizations in the community. A school, for example, should explore possibilities for using computers at libraries, community centers, and other places in the district where they might be available to students on a part-time basis.

In addition, the school's entire system of record keeping ought to take advantage of the efficiencies of technology. Staff members can use computerized data to give greater attention to the needs of individual students. Schools may store this information in a single secure database that users download into other computers, guarding against unauthorized input or access. Such a system makes it easier to maintain attendance records and information pertaining to job and college applications.

When teachers at the West Ottawa Public Schools in Holland, Mich., sign onto the computers at their desks, they have immediate access to student and teacher schedules, daily and monthly attendance information, and the school calendar. They can enter and print report cards, search for materials in the library, and send and receive electronic mail.[55] Each teacher also has a personal phone with voice mail. Eventually, we expect that some school districts will store much of the evidence of the work of students on CD-ROMs that consume little space, enabling a user to see the papers that a student wrote, hear music that a student performed, review a student's play on the basketball court, and observe a student's role in the presentation of a group project.

5. Technology will be a key part of both initial and continuing teacher education to provide teachers with the knowledge and skills they need to integrate technology into the curriculum and to adapt it to instructional strategies. To achieve these ends, school districts will hire teachers who can use technology to obtain information and who can incorporate technology into teaching and learning.

Clearly, shortages of hardware and software have not been the only obstacles to technology's use in the classroom. Technology's role in the instructional program depends largely on whether teachers attain familiarity and facility with technological tools. As matters stand, many teachers lack the confidence and knowledge to infuse their lessons with technology and therefore they tend to ignore technology even when it is available. Eventually, they must learn to work differently if they are to exploit technology's many possibilities for enriching teaching and learning.

For the high school math teacher, for instance, this might mean teaching students new approaches to analyzing data and showing them how to use the kind of mathematical modeling that was not possible to do by hand. Or for the environmental science teacher, it might mean teaching students to use computer models, say, to measure the flow of water released by a dam to predict water quality for a habitat downstream.

Preparation to work with technology ought to be basic to teacher education. Teachers should learn to use technology as an ally in helping students make better use of "inquiry-driven knowledge construction strategies."[56] Colleges and universities that prepare and certify teachers must accept responsibility for ensuring that those who embark on careers in the classroom reach this level. We urge the National Council for Accreditation of Teacher Education and the American Association of Colleges of Teacher Education to use their influence and authority to win compliance from their member institutions for adopting policies that require teachers to reach technological proficiency. Ultimately, high schools should refuse, under most circumstances, to hire onto their faculties those who do not give promise of an ability to use technology in behalf of teaching and learning.

When it comes to veterans already on the faculty, the budget must allow for ongoing training so that they, too, attain technological proficiency. Professional development must accord high priority to this goal. Inservice training in technology can empower an experienced teacher who feels that he or she has missed the computer revolution. In support of this idea, Florida has included in the $165 million in School Technology Incentive Awards that it has granted during the past three years, a proviso that schools spend at least 30 percent of the money on training. We think that veteran teachers, once equipped with the ability to employ technology in their courses, will be more motivated in their work, knowing that they hold dominion over a powerful new tool.

Some school districts find that by using fellow teachers already versed in technology as trainers they can overcome resistance to inservice education, as well as make the training cost-effective. In Boulder Valley School District in Colorado, 21 teachers who received extensive training in using the Internet then trained 80 other staff members; in

Bellevue, Wash., 30 teachers who became technology trainers were paid up to $50 an hour to teach colleagues.[57]

6. Every high school will designate a <u>technology resource person</u> to provide technical assistance and to consult with the staff to assist them in finding the people, information, and materials that they need to make best use of technology.

One of the most valuable expenditure lines in the technology budget may be the one devoted to a resource person in each high school who can consult with staff members on their use of computers and about other technological issues. This work should be part of the person's regular schedule and not heaped on top of other assignments. At medium and large high schools, it ought to be a full-time job. To spend funds on hardware and software without investing in such a person is as shortsighted as buying a car and never taking it out of the garage because you do not learn how to drive.

The person hired into the technological resource position should evince a keen awareness of ways for making technology as cost-effective as possible. The position should, in effect, pay for itself. The technology resource person will be someone distinct from the technicians whom schools also need to provide assistance to keep technology running. For these technical support tasks, schools can recruit student hackers—counterparts to those of another era who acted as audiovisual aides, threading film through projectors and the like. The technology resource person, on the other hand, helps lead the effort to set standards for the use of technology in the school. This person ought to be well connected both literally and figuratively, holding a job that should emerge as one of the most important on any high school faculty.

The best candidate for the position is a certified teacher conversant with issues of teaching and learning. He or she has mastered a disciplinary area and understands curricular and instructional practices, as well as the learning needs of students. On top of this solid educational foundation, the person has built an understanding of technology and can put that expertise to the service of staff members, helping them without intimidating them. Part of this proficiency consists of knowing where colleagues can turn to find appropriate technologies, exemplary models, and experts who can be tapped for further information. ■

The manner in which a high school organizes itself and the ways in which it uses time create a framework that affects almost everything about teaching and learning in the school.

chapter five
ORGANIZATION AND TIME
Restructuring Space and Time for a More Flexible Education

1. High schools will create small units in which anonymity is banished.

2. Each high school teacher involved in the instructional program on a full-time basis will be responsible for contact time with no more than 90 students during a given term so that the teacher can give greater attention to the needs of every student.

3. High schools will develop flexible scheduling that allows for more varied uses of time in order to meet the requirements of the core curriculum.

4. The Carnegie unit will be redefined or replaced so that high schools no longer equate seat time with learning.

5. The high school will reorganize the traditional departmental structure to meet the needs of a more integrated curriculum.

6. Each high school will present alternatives to tracking and to ability grouping, without restricting the range of courses and learning experiences it offers.

7. The academic program will extend beyond the high school campus to take advantage of learning opportunities outside the four walls of the building.

8. Schools will operate on a 12-month basis to provide more time for professional staff development, collegial planning, and the added instruction needed to promote better student learning.

priorities for renewal

1. High schools will create small units in which anonymity is banished. BHS = 592

Students take more interest in school when they experience a sense of belonging. Some students cope in large, impersonal high schools because they have the advantage of external motivation that allows them to transcend the disadvantages of the school's size. Many others, however, would benefit from a more intimate setting in which their presence could be readily and repeatedly acknowledged.

When students become invisible and melt into their surroundings, schools lose the opportunity to engage them fully in academic life. High schools need to organize themselves in ways that make it easier to address the individual needs of students. Teachers should know their students and students, in turn, should know their teachers. Few youngsters remain anonymous either to their peers or to their teachers if a limited number of students encounter a limited number of teachers. Why is it necessary, for instance, for a student to have a different math teacher each year or why should a student attend each course with an entirely different set of classmates?

As a first order of business, each high school should try to limit its enrollment to self-operating units of no more than 600 students. Achieving this objective need not mean assuming the expense of constructing new buildings. Smallness of scale can be created in many ways, even in a structure built to accommodate a large enrollment. House plans and cluster programs, for example, group students into smaller, more intimate units. Such approaches seek to reduce the number of teachers and other students with whom a student comes in contact each day. An organizational approach that produces some kind of school-within-a-school moves toward combating the bigness that shrouds so many youngsters in a cloak of anonymity. "The overwhelming weight of research studies confirm beneficial effects for small high school size and detrimental effects for large high school size," concludes a study by a researcher who examined the literature on the topic.[58]

Many findings confirm the benefits of small size for student attitudes, attendance, participation, and satisfaction, though the evidence is not quite so persuasive that size affects achievement itself. One of the most recent reviews of the data by researchers at the University of Illinois at Chicago echoes most of the earlier conclusions, adding that "females and nonwhite students in particular do better in smaller schools."[59] Scheduling and the length of both the school day and the school year also can serve as allies in creating a more intimate environment. A schedule with fewer class changes lets students spend a longer time with the same students and the same teachers. Lengthening the day or the year can also allow for staggered schedules so that the school accommodates smaller numbers of students at any one time. Another way to help students feel known is to use peer mentors or Personal Adult Advocates (see "School Environment").

Why is it necessary...for a student to have a different math teacher each year or why should a student attend each course with an entirely different set of classmates?

We want to stress, however, that while smallness of scale fosters situations in which teaching and learning more readily thrive, reducing size guarantees nothing in and of itself. Some schools fail to exploit their smallness in ways that give students a sense of belonging. Scaling down represents only a first step in implementing a philosophy that permits students to flourish as individuals and lends credence to the idea that educators care about their schoolwork. Each house or unit within a school that tries to reduce its scale, for instance, should have its own separate faculty so as to limit the number of teachers with whom a student comes in contact during the high school years. Physical demarcations should be employed to underscore the separateness of the units even if this means building a brick wall at the end of a corridor, though the separate units would cooperate to mount programs that require a critical mass of students. Size should be reduced, moreover, in tandem with efforts to treat students fairly and equitably.

2. Each high school teacher involved in the instructional program on a full-time basis will be responsible for contact time with no more than 90 students during a given term so that the teacher can give greater attention to the needs of every student.

Teachers in high schools, unlike their colleagues in elementary schools, do not spend the entire school day with one group of students. Some high school teachers see more than 150 students in their classrooms each day, and most teach at least four or five classes a day. The more students for whom they are responsible, the more difficult it becomes for teachers to get to know those youngsters as individuals and the more tenuous relationships become between teacher and student.

A teacher with a reasonable schedule can spend more time on the instructional needs of each student, taking the time to know the student and to tailor the program for him or her. Furthermore, the teacher has more time for professional development so that he or she can become a better teacher. Our earlier recommendations to provide each student with a Personal Adult Advocate and a Personal Plan for Progress depend on the availability of teachers. Students benefit when their teachers are not burdened with an oppressive workload. Much of what a teacher must do to remain a good teacher involves work outside the classroom. A teacher carrying too heavy a student load cannot readily find time for such vital activities as advising, curriculum writing, instructional preparation, and professional development.

The National Council of Teachers of English points out that when a teacher spends 20 minutes reading, analyzing, and responding to each paper for a class of 25 students, that work alone consumes more than eight hours. A teacher with five classes of 25 students each would spend almost 42 hours responding to an assignment given to each of his or her students. Therefore, if the teacher assigned one paper a week to every student, the 42 hours needed to mark the papers would come on top of a regular work week of about 40 hours, requiring the teacher to work an 80-hour week.[60] The schedule often prevents teachers from giving students feedback on their work.

High schools can restrict work loads through several approaches. During a given term, for instance, a teacher might meet daily with two large classes of 45 students each. In the next term, the teacher might meet with five smaller classes of 18 each. Teachers could use instructional strategies appropriate to the varying sizes of their classes. The idea of flexibility is implicit in this proposal. A maximum workload of 90 students for most high school teachers seems a reasonable goal, with slightly higher or lower averages in some subject areas. As it is, the figure of 90 exceeds the limit of 80 proposed by the National Council of Teachers of English as a goal by the year 2000.[61]

3. High schools will develop flexible scheduling that allows for more varied uses of time in order to meet the requirements of the core curriculum.

High schools should create more flexible schedules—compatible with learning objectives—to make it easier for each student to meet the requirements of the curriculum. What we have in mind is the kind of flexibility that serves learning by organizing instruction in ways more friendly to teaching and learning. Right now, in most high schools, the schedule is frozen, glacier-like, into 50-minute segments that dictate the amount of instructional time devoted to each course, regardless of what would be most appropriate on a particular day.

High schools must examine the basic assumptions about time under which they have long operated—the length of the class period, the length of the school day, and the length of the school year. We agree with the congressionally-sponsored report that concludes: "Unyielding and relentless, the time available in a uniform six-hour day and a 180-day year is the unacknowledged design flaw in American education."[62] So-called "block scheduling" provides extended periods that teachers can devote to one course or, if they choose, split between courses. If, for instance, a team of two teachers shares a block of three consecutive periods they could arrange on a given day for one or the other to use a double period, a practice familiar in some middle level schools. We want to stress, however, that teachers will have to develop new instructional strategies to take advantage of block schedules; they must prepare themselves to do more than lecture twice as long.

Hatboro-Horsham Senior High School in Pennsylvania revamped its daily schedule, doubling class periods from 45 minutes to 90 minutes so that students took only three major courses each term. Students, teachers, and parents in that high school were surveyed before the changes and one year after implementation. Support for the innovations increased among all three groups after people saw what they considered an improved climate for learning in which marks improved and scores on standardized tests rose.[63]

Another schedule variation, the Copernican Plan developed by Joseph M. Carroll, permits the school day to include either one four-hour class each day for 30 days or two two-hour classes that meet for 60 days.[64] Still other approaches allow for configuring the school day and the school year differently, possibly using trimesters or year-round school. Flexible schedules, especially in conjunction with a 12-month school year, can facilitate enrichment, make it easier to offer tutoring, and provide time for students to work on projects—alone, in groups, and in collaboration with teachers. Time will be available for students who lag to catch up and for the ablest students to delve deeper into their studies. Flexibility serves not only the needs of students, but of educators, as well. Teachers and other members of the professional staff can use revamped schedules to pursue professional development, to engage in joint planning, to conduct research, and to work together in the classroom. Elastic schedules can stretch to suit the occasion.

4. The Carnegie unit will be redefined or replaced so that high schools no longer equate seat time with learning.

High schools need release from the rigid time requirements that dictate the length and frequency of classes, serving as barriers to flexibility. Legislatures and state education agencies should reassess prevailing regulations to allow such changes. In this way high schools can more readily base the amount of time devoted to a course on what a student learns and how long it takes him or her to accomplish that learning. A model approach is being fashioned for the seven institutions of the Oregon State System of Higher Education as its Proficiency-Based Admissions Standards System Project takes shape. Beginning in 2001, freshman candidates will gain entrance based on demonstrated proficiency in six content areas and nine process areas rather than on the basis of such traditional time-related measures as the Carnegie unit.

High schools will have to design instructional programs that prepare students for assessments geared to these new standards. Carnegie units are an imperfect

measure of educational accomplishment that equate the number of hours spent sitting in a seat in a classroom with attainment. High schools need better ways to show that students have, in fact, grasped material. At Central Park East Secondary School in New York City, for example, students prepare a portfolio of their work that reveals their competence and performance in 14 curricular areas, ranging from science and technology to ethics and social issues, from school and community service to mathematics, literature, and history.[65]

In breaking the exclusive link with the Carnegie unit, high schools will unambiguously assert that attaining a diploma, for any individual student, may take less than four years or more than four years. Right now, high schools compute graduation rates on the assumption that anyone who does not get a diploma in four years has performed inadequately. High schools, like colleges, must face new realities. In higher education, the average recipient of a bachelor's degree now takes almost five years to complete his or her studies and almost one in eight graduates needs roughly more than six and a half years to get a degree.[66]

High schools need release from the rigid time requirements that dictate the length and frequency of classes, serving as barriers to flexibility.

High schools, too, must acknowledge that what students learn, not the length of time it takes to do the learning, counts most in education. Nonetheless, we expect that most students for the foreseeable future will spend four years completing the studies offered between the ninth and twelfth grades. But just as their counterparts in college, those who take longer should labor under no stigma.

As the Carnegie unit shifts to the background, high schools must make better use of performance assessments, portfolios, exhibits, senior projects, and criterion-referenced testing to determine that students who get diplomas meet the standards for a high school education as set out earlier in this report. No single method of assessment ought to serve this purpose. Endorsements might be added to the diploma for each performance-based requirement a student meets, akin to the Regents' endorsement appended to diplomas in New York State for those who pass certain statewide examinations. Our proposal for redefining or replacing the Carnegie unit corresponds closely with our other recommendations for restructuring organization and time. The various recommendations tend to fit together so that each one leans on the other, much as the construction of an arch depends on the tension of every brick supporting that which is adjacent. Any revision of the system of Carnegie units, as we believe essential, must be tied, for example, to changes in assessment methods. If time no longer reigns as the supreme arbiter of educational attainment then high schools must have available other measures to ensure and warrant that students gain productive advantage from high school.

5. The high school will reorganize the traditional departmental structure to meet the needs of a more integrated curriculum.

In fashioning themselves as small versions of colleges, high schools have emulated many practices of higher education, including the idea that they should organize and dispense knowledge subject by subject. This segmentation, now taken for granted, has produced a departmental structure that restricts possibilities for integrated teaching and learning in the high school. Leslie Santee Siskin's study *Realms of Knowledge: Academic Departments in Secondary Schools* observes that "departmental divisions have become potent barriers to schoolwide communications and community" and that "teachers have more in common with geographically distant colleagues in the same subject than they may with colleagues in the same school."[67] The academic department, as an organizing theme for this approach, shapes the ways that students regard knowledge. As a result, too many young people get diplomas without understanding the connections between and among the various subjects that they have studied.

High schools should reorganize departments to facilitate a multidisciplinary approach to knowledge. They should encourage faculty members to pursue close associations with colleagues in other disciplines, which the existing departmental structure effectively discourages.

Teachers in high schools would probably collaborate more readily if subject area were not the prime way by which they organized themselves. Our goal is to encourage people to reexamine the rationale for departmental structures, not to eliminate disciplines. Indeed, teachers should heighten their knowledge of subject matter and the attendant teaching strategies, but this can occur through disciplinary groups rather than academic departments. Teachers who specialize in the same subject have a natural community of interest and we do not wish to dissuade them from seeking colleagueship according to discipline. Furthermore, we appreciate the need to protect the integrity of teaching and learning from a disciplinary perspective. We hope that such organizations as the National Council of Teachers of Mathematics and the National Council of Teachers of English continue their valuable work in helping teachers sharpen their disciplinary prowess.

Actually, several dimensions of commonality other than subject area link teachers, but these points of connection get less attention than the academic departments. Interdisciplinary coalitions, for example, could enhance efforts to teach critical thinking or to teach problem solving or to use experiential education or cooperative learning or to group students without regard to grade level. In a high school with a house plan or one that uses schools-within-a-school, teachers might orient themselves according to these organizational missions. They could also pursue colleagueship with those who employ a similar pedagogy, as, say, teaching in seminars. The advent of technology may facilitate these various efforts to blur disciplinary demarcations. A computer terminal allows both teachers and students to draw on information from many disciplines that they can use to carry out multidisciplinary projects.

In another approach, each team that presents an interdisciplinary curriculum can function as a kind of mini-department. This could bring together, say, teachers collaborating to convey the art, literature, history, and science of an era or a locale. Working in consultation with each other and sometimes teaching together in the same classroom, these teachers might help students to integrate their learning. A social studies teacher could teach about the history and economics of the Great Depression, a science teacher could teach about the land and weather conditions that forced the migration of the Okies, and an art teacher and an English teacher could teach about the projects sponsored by the Works Progress Administration for painters and writers of the era.

It is time to act on the reality that much of the learning of young people occurs outside the school and that it has credibility.

High schools can build on the approach taken by Hampshire College in Massachusetts, which set out at its origin in 1958 to form an educational institution unencumbered by departments that are defined narrowly by disciplines. A goal was to foster inquiry-based learning that would encourage students to interpret and apply knowledge across the disciplines. Thus, Hampshire's academic program organizes itself around four broad units—the Schools of Natural Science, Social Science, Humanities and Arts, and Communications and Cognitive Science.

6. Each high school will present alternatives to tracking and to ability grouping, without restricting the range of courses and learning experiences it offers.

One of the most important ways that a high school respects its students is by having high academic expectations for all of them. When a school assigns some students to courses with watered-down content, it transmits an unmistakable message to them: The school does not view them as capable of performing higher level work. Little is expected of these students as they are consigned to a dead-end journey, pursuing courses that are pale imitations of the more meaningful courses available to others. Jeannie Oakes, who studied tracked classes in 25 schools, concluded that "students in some classes had markedly different access to knowledge and learning experiences from students in other classes."[68]

High schools that continue to use tracking as a technique for providing some students with a second-rate education will not have a place in the educational future that we envision. Educators should begin raising expectations by doing more to group students heterogeneously

and by not offering substandard courses. We recognize that students, in turn, must rise to meet new challenges if high schools are going to expect more of them. In schools that persist in grouping students by ability levels, the work offered to those assigned to all groups should be challenging and substantial. Schools must exercise special vigilance to prevent grouping from serving as a form of racial segregation.

High schools also raise expectations when they throw open the doors to virtually all courses and end the exclusivity usually associated with honors and Advanced Placement courses. This does not mean obliterating or even diluting such offerings, but making them less restrictive by no longer reserving seats only for students with records of high achievement. The learning goals of the courses should in no way be reduced. We envision a policy under which high schools will open the most demanding courses to all students and will thoroughly describe the expectations and grading standards to them before they enroll in these courses. Students who accede to the academic expectations will get the chance to take the course.

We expect that schools will provide tutoring and other instructional support to enhance chances for success and that teachers will adapt instructional strategies to meet the needs of the students, which is no less than they should do for all students in all high school courses. Alternatives to tracking and ability grouping can take other forms, as well. When teachers organize students into learning groups, as should sometimes happen, diversity can be a criterion to determine the composition of such groups. Students can learn from each other when those of varying backgrounds work together in the same learning group. They bring a multitude of perspectives to situations that might otherwise be more narrowly focused.

7. The academic program will extend beyond the high school campus to take advantage of learning opportunities outside the four walls of the building.

When high schools try to restrict the worthwhile learning of students to what occurs in the building, as now happens, they deprive students of many opportunities away from the school itself that could augment and extend formal learning. It is time to act on the reality that much of the learning of young people occurs outside the school and that it has credibility. For years, high schools have made minimal use of programs that reach beyond the four walls of the classroom: work-study, independent learning, distance learning, apprenticeships, mentorships, internships, job shadowing, independent study, field trips, travel, courses at colleges, student-conducted research.

High schools should reorganize departments to facilitate a multidisciplinary approach to knowledge. They should encourage faculty members to pursue close associations with colleagues in other disciplines, which the existing departmental structure effectively discourages.

High schools should incorporate these approaches and others extensively into the education of students. The setting in which learning occurs—as measured by seat time—will matter less when high schools break free of the restrictions imposed on them by the Carnegie unit. Students should have the opportunity to demonstrate the value of credible learning experiences, wherever they occur. The spread of technology opens a host of possibilities for achieving this objective. A student at a computer, for example, may tap into the collection of a library 100 miles away or carry out a joint project with students in another state. Moreover, the student might pursue a course from a computer in his or her bedroom, turning in a paper to the teacher by e-mail and receiving feedback in the same way. Technology allows students to collaborate with peers in the next classroom or even in a classroom in another country.

Part of the reluctance to extend learning to other settings involves an unwillingness to trust students who are out of sight. And, indeed, some young people do lack the maturity to persist with the lesson unless the teacher lurks nearby to monitor them. The usual studies in the classroom fail to engage all students, however, and often lessons go

unlearned anyway. High schools must begin to explore how students can learn—singly and in groups—away from traditional high school settings and with a sense of mission that keeps them from squandering the opportunity.

8. Schools will operate on a 12-month basis to provide more time for professional staff development, collegial planning, and the added instruction needed to promote better student learning.

Current scheduling arrangements require that teachers squeeze all their work into about 9 months. Instead, it should be spread over 12 months and teachers should be available to schools throughout the year, attending to tasks inside and outside the classroom. This should be a long-range goal of all school systems, though we realize that fiscal constraints will slow down attempts to expand the calendar. Some high school students almost certainly will need days added to their schooling so they can meet the more rigorous academic expectations linked to higher standards. In addition, the summer months should be available for curriculum writing, staff development, team planning, and independent projects carried out by teachers. None of the duties of restructuring, however, should result in a reduction of the contact time that teachers have with students.

The availability of year-long contracts need not mean that every teacher works a 12-month schedule each year or gets paid a 12-month salary. A school system might choose to engage, say, only one-fourth of its teachers on a full-year contract annually, rotating different groups of teachers through these year-round assignments. We envision a series of contracts of varying lengths in force at any one time. An employment schedule of this sort also should allow for hiring part-time faculty members to the extent that they can fill unmet needs. High schools must be free to employ those whose backgrounds best suit the work to be done so long as they are qualified for the work. This may mean, for example, hiring some people on a part-time basis if they have abilities that are needed by the school and letting others work flexible schedules with unusual configurations of working time. Also, some teachers might share assignments so that they have time available for child care or other responsibilities. What counts most is assembling a faculty that adapts itself to the learning needs of students. ■

A Accountability demands that a high school have a set of objectives and assess and report the extent to which they are met. The purpose of this accountability is to ensure that teaching and learning serve the needs of students to the fullest extent.

chapter six

ASSESSMENT AND ACCOUNTABILITY
Individual, Collective, and Institutional Outcomes

1. The high school will assess the academic progress of students in a variety of ways so that a clear and valid picture emerges of what they know and are able to do.

2. The school will review each student's Personal Progress Plan continually and indicate the extent of progress toward graduation and postsecondary transition options.

3. High schools will guarantee that students can meet performance standards in entry-level jobs. Recent graduates who fail to meet these basic standards will have the opportunity to return to school for additional studies.

4. Each high school will report annually to the community, disclosing schoolwide assessment results and other pertinent information.

5. At least once every five years, each high school will convene a broadly-based external panel to offer a Public Description of the school, a requirement that could be met in conjunction with the evaluations of state, regional, and other accrediting groups.

6. Students will evaluate teachers and instruction on an ongoing basis in a variety of ways, providing regular feedback with regard to how effectively student learning goals are met.

7. Supervision of teachers will be thorough and ongoing, making use of the expertise of master teachers as well as administrators.

8. Principals and other administrators will use the highest standards of teaching as the criteria against which to evaluate teachers for determining their continued employment.

9. The high school staff will assess the principal and the administrative team's performance periodically in a variety of ways, providing regular feedback with regard to how effectively school goals are met.

53

priorities for renewal

1. The high school will assess the academic progress of students in a variety of ways so that a clear and valid picture emerges of what they know and are able to do.

Assessments of student work should provide a rich collection of information that reflects on a student's progress in moving through the high school curriculum. Any single method of assessment, however valid, will not capture the full landscape of achievement that ought to be on view for each student. Furthermore, for assessment to depict a student's academic growth, it must not be static. Assessment, in other words, should more closely resemble a videotape than a single snapshot.

This kind of assessment calls for portfolios, performance tasks, and other examples of a student's accomplishments that are indistinguishable from actual classroom assignments. More traditional examinations can enrich the mix, providing a further dimension for assessing the student in the context of the achievements of other students. Standardized tests, particularly those that are criterion-referenced, may serve this purpose. Each student and his or her family must be told explicitly what the youngster knows and can do in relationship to the curriculum. An informed observer examining the evidence should be able to determine the knowledge and skills that a student possesses in connection with completion of a given instructional sequence.

Schools should present assessment results in ways that are useful to parents, college admissions officers, personnel managers, and the student. The assessments must be rigorous so that people can have confidence in them and they should also allow for interpretations of the findings as they apply to individual students. A young person, for example, who aspires to a job in the world of theater should be represented by some assessments that speak to the student's interests, accomplishments, and potential in the theater. Use of these various alternative assessments, incidentally, will require that teachers take a far more active role in assessment. It is one thing, for example, to administer a norm-referenced test that automatically yields a simple reading level score and quite another to oversee and rate an actual performance. High standards of technical quality demand that teachers prepare themselves carefully for this role and carry it out with great diligence. Many teachers will surely need training to construct and use alternative assessments properly.

2. The school will review each student's Personal Progress Plan continually and indicate the extent of progress toward graduation and postsecondary transition options.

Assessment results should show a student's progress toward fulfilling the learning goals associated with a diploma. The student's own Personal Plan for Progress (see "Curriculum") provides a touchstone against which to document individual progress. The plan should indicate the point along a continuum at which the student's achievement stands at any given time. A high school can assist this effort by identifying levels of accomplishment so that youngsters and their families can gauge the progress of students toward graduation, knowing at any interval what remains to be learned or accomplished. The objectives in the personal plan should link themselves to standards identified by the school. Assessments must validly reflect the expectations for graduation as they appear in the curriculum, emphasizing the symbiotic nature of curriculum and assessment. In this way, the high school can help each student tailor a curriculum to his or her own needs, while honoring the curricular requirements that apply to all students.

Assessments of student work should provide a rich collection of information that reflects on a student's progress in moving through the high school curriculum.

As a result of its transitional nature, the Personal Plan for Progress should connect the student's academic progress to the future. A personal plan is incomplete if it looks no further than the day that the high school confers a diploma. That point marks a beginning, not an end. High school itself provides a passageway into adulthood and students should use the time en route to think about their personal goals. Some students may make definitive decisions about the future, while others may have only the vaguest notion of what they expect to do upon completing high school. The plan for progress should embody these personal visions.

MCAS

A student proposing to enter a premedical program at a four-year college, for instance, will be served by a plan different from that of a student who expects to become an apprentice plumber immediately after high school—though some of their courses may overlap. In any event, the student's plan ought to help make the transition from high school as smooth as possible.

3. High schools will guarantee that students can meet performance standards in entry-level jobs. Recent graduates who fail to meet these basic standards will have the opportunity to return to school for additional studies.

A high school must stand behind the product of its efforts, namely, the student to whom it awards a diploma. The granting of that credential should signal that the young adult can move on successfully to life's next phase. Yet, employers have raised serious questions about the abilities of new graduates to perform the jobs that they enter from high school. The refrain is all too familiar as personnel managers describe the deficiencies of 18 and 19-year-olds who cannot do simple arithmetic and lack the skills to write literate sentences. Employers further complain about newly-minted high school graduates who do not understand that they must arrive for work on time, treat customers and fellow employees courteously, and dress and groom themselves in socially acceptable ways. A survey of 4,000 private employers in 1994 found that in hiring new non-supervisory or production workers the companies valued above all else the applicant's attitude and communications skills.[69]

Automobiles and other industrial products carry warranties. Buyers can get them fixed or replaced if they do not work properly. We understand the difference between inanimate objects and human beings, but that does not excuse high schools from the obligation to guarantee the quality of the young people they educate. If a graduate lacks the foundation skills, basic academic knowledge, and reasonable attitudes required in an entry-level job then his or her education has apparently been inadequate. We recommend in this report (see "Relationships") that high schools form close ties with business.

For their own credibility in such partnerships, high schools must evince more concern about the quality of their graduates. Using the SCANS documents as a guide (see "Curriculum"), the high school should ensure that students are taught the competencies and skills deemed necessary for entry-level employment. Students, however, should identify jobs that most interest them because the 20 areas of competency and 17 areas of foundation skills vary in the degree to which they apply in different job settings and a high school cannot be expected to equip each young person for every possible entry-level job in the economy.

A dissatisfied employer should document the new graduate's shortcomings in a report to the high school. Former students should also have the chance to refer themselves back to the high school by showing that their job search has failed because they were not properly prepared. If, according to reasonable standards for entry-level jobs, the young person's education proves deficient then the high school must arrange for the graduate to get the attention he or she needs. This can be done through a regular class at a high school or community college, independent directed study, a special remedial program, or in some other appropriate manner.

Returning graduates must be willing to learn. Those for whom attitude and deportment have proven to be a problem may merit no more than a meeting with a counselor to review the personal qualities that the SCANS report identifies as basic for a responsible employee—namely, attributes that include good job attendance, punctuality, friendliness, appropriate responses to situations, self-control, and showing an interest in what others say and do. As a result of this extra attention, the diploma holder should return to a job for which he or she was already hired or try to find a first job. Implicit in this recommendation, of course, is the notion that a high school will not award a diploma in the first place to a student who has not advanced far enough to deserve it.

4. Each high school will report annually to the community, disclosing schoolwide assessment results and other pertinent information.

While it is important to assess individual students so that their academic progress may be known, it is equally vital to disclose how the school as a whole fares. Parents, for example, need sufficient overall knowledge about a high school to judge whether it is the best place for their youngsters. "The publication of information about school performance that is required for accountability provides families with the basis for informed choice," says the Consortium on Productivity in the Schools.[70] Annual reports issued by high schools should include data relating to such concerns as average daily attendance, teacher absenteeism, expenditures, student turnover, statewide and local assessment results, dropout and graduation rates, student participation in cocurricular activities, college acceptances, and where graduates stand several years after high school. Several states now require such reports. Littleton High School, near Denver, has produced an exemplary report to the community, cramming it full of graphs, bar charts, pie charts, and school-administered survey results that paint a vivid picture of trends in the school.

While it is important to assess individual students so that their academic progress may be known, it is equally vital to disclose how the school as a whole fares.

In presenting the results of schoolwide assessments, the annual report should offer a kind of achievement profile for the student body. These various forms of measurement ought to provide a composite view of academic achievement in the high school. For example, the schoolwide report might tell the degree to which tenth graders can write an analytical paper on an appropriate literary theme or the extent to which eleventh graders can conduct a specified experiment in a chemistry laboratory or how twelfth graders perform on a national mathematics examination.

High schools should make copies of these reports available in the main office. In addition, the school can offer oral presentations of the report. Officials in some states that use this kind of reporting say it serves as a tool for the repair work crucial to school improvement. In Virginia, for instance, some district superintendents require their schools to link the reports to the state's Outcome Accountability Project, and reports in Florida use data to track each school's progress toward meeting needs identified in the school's improvement plan.[71] The

California High School Task Force recommended in 1992 that student performance data be provided in order to hold schools accountable for the ongoing improvement of students.[72]

5. At least once every five years, each high school will convene a broadly-based external panel to offer a Public Description of the school, a requirement that could be met in conjunction with the evaluations of state, regional, and other accrediting groups.

High schools will gain from knowing how outsiders view them. The regional accreditation to which some high schools voluntarily submit provides input of this sort. High schools that already participate in this kind of accreditation process might satisfy this recommendation by augmenting and releasing the report they receive from the accrediting agency. Formal accreditation, however, must change to be more useful to high schools. Accreditors need to concern themselves with the kinds of issues addressed in this report and more closely scrutinize results, particularly as they pertain to the goals of school reform. Until now, accreditation has not fulfilled its potential in regard to the improvement of high schools. A review of the kind we recommend could borrow from the practices of both the regional accrediting groups across the United States and Her Majesty's Inspectorate in Great Britain. Criteria paralleling the goals of school reform will provide benchmarks for the review. The review should culminate in a report that we call a Public Description, which will be produced about every five years to keep up with changes in the student body and the evolving nature of restructuring. A Public Description should devote itself to the day-to-day life of the school and its students. A panel of reviewers would present the Public Description both in printed form and in a public session open to the community as a kind of corporate annual meeting. Members of the panel, comprising six to eight visitors, should include parents, teachers from other schools, public officials, and members of citizens' groups. A student who attends a high school elsewhere ought to be on the panel.

6. Students will evaluate teachers and instruction on an ongoing basis in a variety of ways, providing regular feedback with regard to how effectively student learning goals are met.

Instruction at the high school level will improve when teachers gain more insight into how their lessons register on students. This feedback to faculty by students should be ongoing and take various forms. Each high school must find its own ways of gathering such information. However it is done, what counts most is that students have an opportunity to express their opinions about instruction and that teachers use what they learn to bring about improvement. Faculty members can hold regular feedback sessions to elicit student input. They should interview students to determine the worth of the instructional techniques and materials used in courses.

What do students believe that they have learned? The answers to this simple but profound question can be revealing. In addition to asking students about academics, high schools should also inquire into the extent to which teachers and others in the school contribute to the growth and development of youngsters outside the classroom—in cocurricular activities and advising, for instance.

Anonymous evaluations of teachers by students can also be carried out through a standard form that teachers distribute upon the completion of courses. Questions should tap into the reactions of students to their experiences. Various questions would serve this purpose. Examples can be found among the questions asked of tenth graders in a study sponsored by the U.S. Department of Education—whether students get along with teachers, whether discipline is fair, whether teaching is good, whether teachers are interested in students, and whether teachers listen to what students say.[73] The teacher should collect the completed forms for his or her personal edification, sharing the responses with others only if he or she chooses. Presumably, the teacher will study the responses and reflect upon them, thinking about the implications for teaching and learning.

7. *Supervision of teachers will be thorough and ongoing, making use of the expertise of master teachers as well as administrators.*

Good supervision helps people improve their work by giving them insight into their job performance. Everyone, regardless of experience or status level, can benefit from such input. We distinguish between supervision, a function to assist teachers with their ongoing professional growth, and evaluation, which concerns itself with the continued

employment of teachers. This recommendation has to do with supervision and the next recommendation in this section deals with evaluation. High schools can in most cases separate the supervisory function from the evaluative, making supervision more successful because teachers could more readily reveal themselves and their needs to peers who they know are not assessing their performance for purposes of continued employment.

Supervision assumes special importance in an era of restructuring because of the demands put on educators by reforms that call for fresh approaches. High schools require new systems of teacher supervision more closely tied to the needs of restructuring. Such concerns have guided several projects that hold promise for schools

> ## Supervision assumes special importance in an era of restructuring because of the demands put on educators by reforms that call for fresh approaches.

seeking ways to improve supervision. We have in mind, for example, the activities of the National Board of Professional Teaching Standards, the Interstate New Teacher Assessment and Support Consortium, the National Association of State Directors of Teacher Education and Certification, the National Council for Accreditation of Teacher Education, and the Educational Testing Service's Praxis III Performance Assessment. In addition, there are more specific efforts such as the one being developed and tested by the Center for Research on Educational Accountability and Teacher Evaluation at Western Michigan University under the sponsorship of the U.S. Department of Education. The Center has a pilot project under way in Dallas, where an aim is to help teachers learn how well they serve their students and in what respects they need to improve their teaching performance.[74]

More time must be devoted to supervision if it is to have greater impact on school improvement. As matters now stand, supervision ranks low on the priority list of tasks assigned to principals and other administrators.

They have too many other, more pressing matters with which to deal. Under optimum conditions, a principal should supervise the work of no more than 10 teachers a year, in light of the time necessary to observe in the classroom, discuss the lessons before and after they are taught, and write reports on the whole process. Yet, supervisory loads are heavier because few high schools authorize enough people to take on this time-consuming task.

Implicit in the hierarchical model of organization that has long prevailed in schools is the idea that only the principal or some other administrator can properly critique the performance of teachers and help them improve their craft. We propose to lighten the load by including master teachers among the supervisors. They are qualified to assume this role and should receive work schedules that enable them to carry it out. Administrators and master teachers, sharing responsibility for supervision, should try to put each teacher through a cycle of supervision at least once every three years. Supervisors— whether they are peers or administrators—should increasingly act as coaches to those whose work they observe, focusing on the continuing development of the teacher's knowledge and skills.[75] We expect reluctance at first from some teachers who are asked to open themselves up to peers and from some veteran teachers who are asked to supervise peers. Nonetheless, schools should move in this collegial direction to avoid situations that lead to spotty and inadequate supervision of teaching by administrators who lack sufficient time for the job.

8. Principals and other administrators will use the highest standards of teaching as the criteria against which to evaluate teachers for determining their continued employment.

Students in every high school in the land deserve good teachers. Only with such teachers can high schools assure themselves of a measure of success in pursuing the reform agenda set down in the pages of this report. This means that evaluations related to the continued employment of teachers—whether seeking tenure, already on tenure, or a candidate for renewal of a contract—must deem mediocrity as unacceptable. We want to underscore the fundamental role that teachers play in determining the quality of the education that students receive and in deciding whether the high school itself merits the approbation of accreditors and the public.

Principals and other administrators who evaluate teachers must recognize that no aspect of their work has greater importance. School districts should support principals with policies that allow them to give this task the time and priority that it merits. The process of evaluation must exhibit fairness every step of the way to ensure the careful scrutiny to which teachers are entitled on questions of continued employment and to assure the public that the school regards this responsibility with utmost seriousness.

Evaluation should never be arbitrary, capricious, or prejudicial. Leading organizations including the National Association of Secondary School Principals, the National School Boards Association, the American Association of Supervisors and Administrators, the National Education Association, and the American Federation of Teachers have documentation that principals and others can use to establish criteria by which to evaluate teaching quality. The process must protect the jobs of good teachers and act effectively to rid high schools of teachers who are less than good and whose continued employment will not benefit students.

9. The high school staff will assess the principal and the administrative team's performance periodically in a variety of ways, providing regular feedback with regard to how effectively school goals are met.

Those who work in a high school should periodically assess the principal and other administrators, examining how effectively they function as a team. This input by teachers and other professional educators will provide the principal and his or her team with a sounding board against which to judge their performance. The importance of judging the work of the entire administrative team and not just the principal is emphasized by a study sponsored by the National Association of Secondary School Principals. It found that principals in "productive" high schools involved administrative teams in problem solving, planning, and decision making, though, incidentally, the principal reserved veto power over team decisions.[76] The opinions of teachers do not necessarily give a full estimate of the principal's work, but certainly these views deserve careful consideration by administrators.

The process for assessing the principal and the administrative team, like the procedures that we propose for students who fill out evaluation forms on teachers, should be anonymous and confidential. High schools should not ask teachers to sign their names to the evaluation forms. We hope that the principal and members of the administrative team use the information to affirm favorable aspects of their performance and to identify areas that need improvement. Administrators can benefit greatly from teacher input, especially in regard to actions having to do with change, encouragement of the professional growth of the staff, provision of supplies and resources, use of evaluation criteria as applied to teachers, overall management, and leadership. ■

A WEB
OF SUPPORT

We see the priorities for renewal that we have just discussed as a framework for restructuring high schools. The successful implementation of these recommendations will depend on acting on several fronts, a substantial challenge, indeed. The work of renewal will be facilitated by efforts in the areas that support the framework. Like the strands of a spider's web, each of these supporting areas reaches into and affects the framework of the high school. The individual strands of this web of support comprise professional development, diversity, governance, resources, ties to higher education, and relationships. What happens in each of these areas will have an impact on the priorities.

Professional development, for example, will be a source of the knowledge and skills that enable educators to carry out the recommendations in most of the other areas in this report. Professional development affects curriculum, instructional strategies, school environment, technology, organization and time, and assessment and accountability. In much the same way, the other parts of this web of support lend strength to efforts to bring the priorities to life. One can readily see, for instance, how reforms involving governance or resources will affect all the areas of the framework discussed in the first part of this report. The interdependency indicates the need for systemic reform in high schools. Reformers must recognize that changes and improvements taken in one area will inevitably affect other aspects of the school's operation. This means that advocates of educational restructuring should always be aware, even when they try to change only one area at a time, of the wider consequences of their actions. ■

Teachers, administrators, and other educators who are part of a high school must regard their own learning as integral to their professional role. This is especially so at a time when roles will change in conjunction with restructuring. The school district should help educators to create a learning community in which substantive professional development, linked primarily to content knowledge and to instructional strategies, plays an ongoing part in their work.

chapter seven

PROFESSIONAL DEVELOPMENT
Helping School Staff Members Fulfill Their Potential

*State
Requirement
Odee
recertification*

- District Plan
- Inservice Days
- Training Dau
- Program adoption
- Grants -
    - Title VI
    - Eisenhower
    - Gifted Ed
- Advanced Placement training

1. Every high school will be a learning community for teachers and for the other professionals it employs.

2. Each educator will create a Personal Learning Plan that addresses his or her need to grow, stressing knowledge and skills related to improved student learning.

   The high school—with the help of the school district—will provide adequate funding, time, and other resources to ensure that professional development is a continuous, ongoing process.

4. The principal of a high school, as a model for the staff, will pursue his or her own ongoing professional growth while helping to lead the professional development for the entire school.

5. The support staff of a high school—secretaries, custodians, cafeteria workers, and others—will also be encouraged and assisted in their own career growth and drawn into the larger school community as adults who can promote the well-being of students.

a web of support

1. Every high school will be a learning community for teachers and for the other professionals it employs.

Teachers must see themselves as part of a learning community in which their own professional improvement connects itself to the growth of their students. Attempts by teachers to improve should not be viewed, however, solely in terms of individual prescriptions dispensed without considering the well-being of the entire faculty. Some professional development will address individual needs, but we expect a high school's faculty mainly to approach professional development in a collegial spirit so that the community of learners works together to make the school better. A learning community values the intellectual development of all its members and provides mechanisms to foster that growth, especially at a time when the school is trying to alter long-established practices and policies. The dynamics of the process of teaching and learning demand flexibility of practitioners so as to avoid applying yesterday's solution to tomorrow's problem. "The development of a professional community in a particular school, or the lack of it, can have implications for other reform efforts," notes the Center on Organization and Restructuring of Schools. "Our research suggests that human resources—such as openness to improvement, trust and respect, teachers having knowledge and skills, supportive leadership, and socialization—are more critical to the development of professional community than structural conditions."[77]

A learning community values the intellectual development of all its members and provides mechanisms to foster that growth, especially at a time when the school is trying to alter long-established practices and policies.

The learning community should organize its professional development around the goals that the school establishes for its students so that teachers equip themselves to help students meet these aims. The success of restructuring depends on good professional development, a point affirmed by researchers at the federally-funded North Central Regional Educational Laboratory, which stated: "Again and again we attempt to implement new instructional innovations, yet fail to provide teachers with ongoing opportunities to study, reflect upon, and apply the research on teaching and learning."[78] Teacher learning can serve as a vehicle for building a more collegial staff in which collaboration in pursuit of professional objectives becomes the norm rather than the exception. Such programs should promote the idea of professionals joining together to stretch themselves. Lasting bonds formed among participants will make it easier to enlist and retain people in joint endeavors aimed at school improvement.

2. Each educator will create a Personal Learning Plan that addresses his or her need to grow, stressing knowledge and skills related to improved student learning.

A Personal Learning Plan will facilitate self-appraisal by teachers. Ideally, the plan will emanate from the teacher's own awareness of the steps needed to improve or simply to keep pace. This means periodically taking stock of one's professional knowledge and abilities and making necessary adjustments. The learning plan for teachers, like the Personal Plan for Progress that we propose for each student, endures as a living document throughout one's association with the school, continually altered in recognition of changing circumstances. Teachers must develop strategies for dealing with the many evolving aspects of their work. They should draw on portfolios that they maintain of their teaching activities, the observations of supervisors and colleagues, the appraisals that students make of teachers (see "Assessment and Accountability"), and their own professional reflections.

In no way do we intend that a teacher's Personal Learning Plan have punitive connotations. To the contrary, the aim is salutary. Self-reflection becomes more effective when pursued in a formal and systematic way. The continual reformulation of the learning plan should lead an educator to pursue improvement in ways besides taking additional university courses, though this is one route to professional growth. We also have in mind such activities as seminars, workshops, training sessions, and independent readings that open new intellectual doors. In addition, professional and disciplinary organizations offer teachers many opportunities to obtain publications and to participate in conferences designed to bolster knowledge and skills. A teacher who maintains a Personal Learning Plan will have a kind of road map that leads to a more fulfilling and satisfying career, making lifelong learning more than an empty phrase for teachers.

3. The high school—with the help of the school district—will provide adequate funding, time, and other resources to ensure that professional development is a continuous, ongoing process.

Many of the changes called for in this report cannot be brought about unless professional development becomes integral to the job description of teachers. Not all teachers have the preparation they need to undertake the initiatives proposed for school improvement. The peril that inadequate staff development poses for school reform was noted by the Consortium for Policy Research in Education: "We saw little by way of staff development that appeared up to the challenges ahead. Most staff development we found was fragmented and piecemeal, identified and delivered by persons distant from the classroom, and with little, if any, explicit connection to strengthening academic instruction."[79]

A comprehensive plan should guide all personal and group professional development so that the investment of time and money reaps dividends.

School systems can demonstrate a commitment to improved student learning by ensuring that sufficient funds are available for professional development. We recommend that each district set aside at least 5 percent of its annual budget for professional development, a portion to remain constant through good and bad fiscal times. Expenditures for this purpose, including the value of salary increments tied to professional development, now range from just under 2 percent to just over 5 percent, according to various estimates.[80]

Yet, money alone, as much as it is needed for professional development, will not automatically remedy the problems of the past. Teachers need time to engage in activities associated with their growth, especially in an era in which knowledge expands exponentially. A comprehensive plan should guide all personal and group professional development so that the investment of time and money reaps dividends. The 12-month contract that we advocate (see "Organization and Time") will help make available more time for professional development so that teachers no longer have to squeeze these activities into a restricted calendar. Other ways to give teachers more time for professional development include the use of team teaching and collaborative planning and the use of substitute teachers who fill the same spots on a regular basis, acting as part-time members of a team. The key here is that policymakers and educators not consider professional development as a one-shot effort. A high school should formulate a comprehensive, long-range strategy for the growth of its staff so that the sessions add up to something more than a loose collection of unconnected inservice meetings.

4. The principal of a high school, as a model for the staff, will pursue his or her own ongoing professional growth while helping to lead the professional development for the entire school.

Like musicians in a symphony orchestra, the many teachers on a high school faculty play different parts in order to produce what should flow forth as a smooth, coherent education for students. The principal, ideally, acts as both conductor and orchestrator, leading and inspiring the players while identifying ways for each to play a part that contributes to the excellence of the overall performance. The best principals are maestros whose sense of timing and ability to lead stamp an indelible mark on the ensemble that we call a faculty. Such a person is a reader and a thinker, a teacher and a learner, as well as a provocateur, capable of framing issues in ways that prod members of the faculty to seek excellence. This kind of principal, no matter how busy, finds time to remain on the cutting edge of the knowledge regarding best high school practices. Such a principal constantly monitors his or her own performance and finds ways to improve it, writing a Personal Learning Plan, just as the teachers do.

In calling upon the principal to look after his or her own professional development while simultaneously assisting others on the high school staff with theirs, we realize that we set our expectations high. But this concomitant responsibility must be inherent in the principalship if those who administer high schools are to act as agents for change. Principals, like the teachers around them, must keep growing. In this regard, principals can be models. We perceive the principal as a person who in the traditional and finest sense is a devotee of learning. Good principals should be practitioner-scholars.

5. The support staff of a high school—secretaries, custodians, cafeteria workers, and others—will also be encouraged and assisted in their own career growth and drawn into the larger school community as adults who can promote the well-being of students.

If the students, the teachers, the principal, and other educators in a high school should concern themselves with their own growth, then surely the institution must extend the same philosophy to the support staff. To do otherwise is hypocritical. Secretaries, custodians, cafeteria workers, and others deserve the chance to extend themselves so they can reach their full potential. This approach serves the needs of the school, as well as those of the individual. For example, knowledge of hazardous waste enables a custodian to safeguard the school community in disposing of used materials from the chemistry laboratory. Enhanced computer skills allow a secretary to attempt tasks like desktop publishing that could serve the school well. Greater familiarity with nutritional principles lets a food supervisor promote the health of those who eat in the cafeteria. Members of the support staff who keep abreast of the elements of school improvement better appreciate the changes in the school and can contribute from their own areas of specialization. For most members of the support staff, we suspect that this kind of enhancement will result in doing a better job and finding deeper satisfaction in their work.

Obviously, a career ladder in a school has just so many rungs on which to accommodate support staff. A high school is not a multinational corporation with a host of positions to fill. Members of the support staff can end up outgrowing their jobs. Therefore, it is worth considering how the school might serve their evolving needs. Princeton University, for instance, offers a program that enables support employees to upgrade their skills and move to more demanding positions within the institution. A small number of workers already on the staff at Princeton may join an apprenticeship program that gives them on-the-job training and technical education to qualify them for promotions to more complex jobs within the university. We are reminded of the programs that some school systems, including New York City, have offered to permit teacher aides eventually to become full-fledged teachers. School districts should see how members of the support staff can gain the background to shift positions or at least help them to find such employment outside the district. That, after all, is what growth is supposed to do for people. ∎

An understanding of and respect for diversity should be absorbed into the fabric of each high school, whatever the composition of its enrollment. Schools ought to help students to see diversity in its broadest sense as an expression of the American experience. Diversity should be considered in connection with the school's curriculum, instructional practices, and staffing. In the end, education ought to equip students for the interdependency of life in the 21st century.

chapter eight
DIVERSITY
Finding Strength in Differences

all statement
←

1. The principal, the school community, and the school board will promote policies, practices, and decisions that recognize diversity in accord with the core values of a democratic and civil society and within the mission of teaching and learning.

2. The curriculum will expose students to a rich array of viewpoints, perspectives, and experiences.

3. The teachers, adjunct teachers, paraprofessionals, support staff, volunteers, and members of the community who staff the high school will represent a wide array of talents, perspectives, and backgrounds.

4. The school will offer its staff substantive, ongoing professional development to help them deal with issues of diversity.

1. The principal, the school community, and the school board will promote policies, practices, and decisions that recognize diversity in accord with the core values of a democratic and civil society and within the mission of teaching and learning.

A high school demonstrates the values that it represents in many ways. We think that each high school should set out to show that it respects differences among people and try to prevent those differences from obstructing any student's attainments. The high school should enunciate this philosophy as a goal and weave it into the fabric of the institution through policies and practices. It is not simply a matter of encouraging tolerance, but of equipping students to recognize the strengths and advantages of a diverse population. All the students in the school can be enriched by the diversity in their midst. Young people should come to know the world that they will inherit. The school board, by its policies and actions, ought to establish a supportive climate for respecting diversity throughout the district, but high schools need not wait for signals from their boards to act on these matters.

High schools should, if necessary, be islands of tolerance where those whose customs and traditions and ideas might subject them to derision elsewhere can find refuge.

Mention of the word "diversity" these days most often is associated with matters of race and ethnicity. We think it should go even further. The embrace of diversity should also lead to a healthy respect for a broad range of ideas, which, after all, constitute the life blood of any institution devoted to education. The most stable ground in which to anchor an American high school's commitment to diversity is that formed by the fundamental beliefs of this nation as set out in such seminal documents as the Declaration of Independence, the Constitution, and the Bill of Rights. Collectively, these sources and related writings form the spine of this nation's democratic framework. Some people consider such pronouncements as "all men are created equal" as old-fashioned or even trite, but high schools will revivify such words by giving them meaning every moment of the day.

When we speak of recognizing diversity "in accord with the core values of a democratic and civil society," we refer back to such values as those enunciated earlier (see "School Environment"): honesty, dependability, trust, responsibility, tolerance, and respect, for instance. High schools should, if necessary, be islands of tolerance where those whose customs and traditions and ideas might subject them to derision elsewhere can find refuge. A high school's dedication to diversity has limits, though. The school need not impose an unreasonable burden on itself by trying to acknowledge every conceivable shade of difference. Moreover, some differences are antithetical to democratic and civil values and disruptive to the larger school community. The forms of these disruptions range all the way from the actions of students who play radios loudly or intimidate their classmates to those who spew hate or turn to violence. A high school must mobilize itself in fierce opposition to those who engage in such vile activities as race baiting, gay bashing, swastika daubing, or sexual harassment.

2. The curriculum will expose students to a rich array of viewpoints, perspectives, and experiences.

Full treatment of diversity requires that the teaching resources of the school reflect a commitment to inclusion. Publishers have progressed to the point that they produce textbooks and other materials that recognize the backgrounds of a more diverse population. High schools should know about these resources and use the best of them. They should be supplemented by teacher-made materials and guest speakers, allowing for customization to the particular needs of the school. Technology provides a valuable tool in this regard. No student, for instance, should have to imagine how the Rev. Martin Luther King, Jr., sounded and looked when he spoke. Videotape, CD-ROMs, and videodiscs can bring Dr. King to life in classrooms across the land. Similarly, if a teacher wants to guarantee that students understand that blacks fought in the Civil War, the prize-winning film *Glory* can engage even the most recalcitrant student.

Teachers must bear in mind that the curriculum can consist of much more than just the textbooks assigned to each course. To enrich the array of viewpoints, perspectives, and experiences, teachers may draw upon many original and supplementary sources, especially in the social sciences and the humanities. At the same time, teachers should encourage students to exercise their powers of critical judgment so that they understand the difference between fact and opinion and recognize how diverse backgrounds can produce conflicting interpretations. "Writers and researchers have seriously challenged the claims made by positivists that knowledge can be value-free, and they have described the ways in which knowledge claims are influenced by the gender and ethnic characteristics of the knower," says James A. Banks of the Center for Multicultural Education at the University of Washington. He adds that "scholars argue that the human interests and value assumptions of those who create knowledge should be identified, discussed, and examined."[81]

3. The teachers, adjunct teachers, paraprofessionals, support staff, volunteers, and members of the community who staff the high school will represent a wide array of talents, perspectives, and backgrounds.

Students must learn by example that teachers come in all varieties. We do not believe that students learn only from those of their own color or their own ethnic group, but we do think that high schools that fail to strive toward diversity in staffing send a subtle message to students about prospects in this world. Broadening the array of people represented on the staff makes it that much more likely that the school will expose students to people whose life experiences and ways of viewing subject matter vary. As it is, only 12.8 percent of the teachers in public and private elementary and secondary schools in the 1990–91 academic year were members of minority groups, a percentage that is not keeping pace with the growth of minority enrollment.[82] A commitment to diversity should figure in each school system's recruiting and hiring policies. The common denominator for all staff members in their work with students, however, regardless of the backgrounds of staff members, ought to be a dedication to truth and an allegiance to high standards. Students deserve no less. Room should exist within these parameters to ensure that young people receive an education that reflects the real America.

High schools should enlist creativity as a partner in this effort. Technology, for instance, allows for electronic hookups between schools that are 2 miles, 200 miles, or 2,000 miles apart. Almost any school can take advantage of the wonders of technology to pair students in one of its classes with students in a very different kind of school on a joint project. This is not the same as sitting in a classroom together, but it permits a kind of interplay among diverse groups of students that might not otherwise occur. The Internet can help in this regard, but high schools must monitor use of the Internet by their students. Teachers should impress students with the ethical dimensions of their activities on the Internet and make them aware of abhorrent uses of technology by those who disseminate hate and pornography.

4. The school will offer its staff substantive, ongoing professional development to help them deal with issues of diversity.

Some teachers and staff members need special preparation to teach students who differ from those with whom they are most familiar. Educators should inform themselves about the cultural backgrounds of their students and show sensitivity toward the particular needs that may accompany those differences in backgrounds. It follows that teachers ought to help students understand and appreciate the differences among those who inhabit the classroom. All this means that a school will more likely deal with diversity successfully if it provides proper preparation for its staff. This kind of professional development should come during initial teacher training and in continuing inservice education.

The Holmes Group, an organization of leading university-based schools of education, had this to say about the preparation of teachers so that they can deal with diversity in the classroom: "Professional studies should contribute research-based findings on learning differences that stem from cultural backgrounds. Education professionals can be taught procedures for gathering information about children, families, and communities and for assessing their teaching in light of children's preferred learning and the interaction of the school with styles in the home and in the community. The implications for developing a multitude of teaching strategies are implicit..."[83] ■

Enlightened governance is indispensable to reforming education. Boards of education and superintendents are responsible for developing within each high school the capacity to support the very difficult work of school-level change. Responsibility for implementing policies in each school should reside at the school.

chapter nine
GOVERNANCE
Streamlining the Operations of Schools and School Districts

1. Boards of education will essentially follow the model of corporate boards in business and industry. They will take responsibility for adopting goals, policies, and standards of accountability; for approving the district's budget; and for hiring and monitoring the superintendent, who will be free to run day-to-day operations.

2. The superintendent will work collaboratively to build a vision for improving teaching and learning and attaining educational goals. He or she will educate the community about the needs of schools and nurture the development of shared leadership throughout the district.

3. Each high school will establish a site council to work with the principal in reaching decisions to make the school an effective organization for student learning.

a web of support

1. Boards of education will essentially follow the model of corporate boards in business and industry. They will take responsibility for adopting goals, policies, and standards of accountability; for approving the district's budget; and for hiring and monitoring the superintendent, who will be free to run day-to-day operations.

Public-spirited Americans who serve on boards of education deserve the gratitude of their fellow citizens, who sometimes take such service for granted. Some people disparage school boards, an attitude engendered by mis-understandings—on the part of both board members and the general public—over the proper role that these bodies perform. Overall goals, policies, and standards of accountability constitute the proper domain of a school board, which should follow the model of the best corporate boards. For example, the school board should define the duties of top-ranking administrators, oversee the budget, set guidelines for collective bargaining, approve curricular frameworks and standards, and establish policies for collaboration with outside partners. The hiring of a superintendent is the single most important duty of a school board. Then the superintendent, who is, of course, the chief executive of the school system, should be free to oversee the operations of the organization.

The hiring of a superintendent is the single most important duty of a school board.

School boards everywhere should act as shapers of public policy, a challenging and demanding role that takes great preparation. Without such preparation, which clearly is lacking in some cases, members of school boards might not be equipped to discharge their duties responsibly. Parents and other taxpayers expect members of their school boards to concern themselves with matters affecting the big picture, the larger issues of teaching and learning that frame the educational agenda in the community. The details are best left to the superintendent and the education professionals employed to implement and carry out policies. The effectiveness of education in any district depends on the school board speaking with sufficient clarity of purpose and providing enough latitude for professionals to perform the work that they are hired to do.

School board members who follow the tenets that we enunciate here should normally not find it necessary to meet too often or to devote excessive amounts of time to their work. Boards of some of the biggest industrial corporations meet less frequently than some school boards. Between regular meetings, committees of the corporate board take up specific business that would overload the meeting of the full board or matters that need more immediate attention, as, indeed, committees of school boards might do. But, by and large, the ranking officers of the corporation itself are charged with carrying out the policies of the corporate board. We find this paradigm appropriate for school districts.

Yet, a series of studies of school boards since the mid-1980s by the Institute of Educational Leadership reveals that school boards have not adhered to the guidelines just put forward. The studies confirm the obsession of some boards with minutiae and attest to a lack of effectiveness in the very areas that ought to comprise the core activities of school boards—leadership, planning, goal setting, and policy oversight. Furthermore, anonymous, self-administered ratings reveal the ineffectiveness of boards in working with their superintendents to develop a common definition of the role of the school board or to develop education policy.[84]

2. The superintendent will work collaboratively to build a vision for improving teaching and learning and attaining educational goals. He or she will educate the community about the needs of schools and nurture the development of shared leadership throughout the district.

A superintendent should help the school board in an assertive and positive way to form its agenda. As the district's top professional employee, he or she should act to keep board members abreast of educational trends and knowledgeable about leading issues in teaching and learning. In similar fashion, the superintendent must collaborate with ranking administrators in the central office and the schools to ensure that the mechanisms of governance operate smoothly, efficiently, and in the best interests of children. It falls to the superintendent to show principals that the district values them. A wise superintendent will make principals part of the inner circle, recognizing their need to feel they have a stake in the action and taking advantage of their informed input in reaching important decisions. The best superintendents develop an attitude of mutual trust and respect with and among principals and central administrators. In part, this means giving administrators latitude to make their own decisions in meeting goals that have previously been agreed upon and intervening only when asked or if commitments are not being met.

In this era of restructuring, a person unprepared to govern a school system in the midst of change should not hold a superintendency. The superintendent ought to be a visionary, someone who believes in educational improvement and can educate and persuade others to follow paths leading toward better teaching and learning. Few school districts can afford to adhere to the status quo. In fact, the superintendent's unwillingness or inability to lead change has accounted for the failure of school improvement in some districts. Because no superintendent can carry out the tasks of restructuring unaided, he or she needs to nurture the leadership of others and provide opportunities for them to take responsibility for various restructuring activities.

At this historic juncture, the superintendent must recognize the primacy of leadership that is explicitly educational. The superintendent's astuteness will do much to determine whether or not the district realizes its academic goals. The superintendent cannot carry forth his or her duties from the sanctuary of an ivory tower, untouched by the political combat that rages below. To win support for the policies that he or she wants to implement, the superintendent must join the debate, doing everything possible to act as an effective advocate in order to win support for restructuring policies. The courage of others to do battle against naysayers will be bolstered by the superintendent's ability during these debates to keep the focus on student learning as the paramount concern of the school system.

3. Each high school will establish a site council to work with the principal in reaching decisions to make the school an effective organization for student learning.

Governance at the building level should be carried out largely by those associated with the particular school, operating within parameters set down by the school board and monitored from the district level by the super-

intendent or a representative of the superintendent. A site council, working closely with the principal, can identify educational needs, set goals, and reach decisions in line with the policies set by the central school board, particularly in regard to budget, curriculum, and allocation of staff. A shift of responsibility to the school level conforms with the spirit of this entire report, which calls on students, parents, teachers, and administrators to take greater personal responsibility for making education effective.

We do not wish to be prescriptive about membership on school site councils except to say that the principal and possibly some other administrators, as well as some of the building's teachers certainly belong on the council. Others to consider for membership are students, parents, support staff, and neighborhood residents without children in the school. Some existing site councils also draw members from among public officials and representatives of business and industry. A high school might additionally weigh the advisability of including on the council those from higher education and from the lower schools. Members of the council, just as those who serve on the school board, will most likely need some special preparation for the task. "The transition to SBM (site-based management) involves extensive change in roles that must be accompanied by intensive development of new skills and capacities," the Consortium for Policy Research in Education points out, adding that "it will not succeed unless development is planned and resources are provided."[85]

Even as we recommend site-based management, we do not want to hold it out as a panacea for what ails schools. In fact, what most justifies the approach is the assumption that a site council will predicate its very existence on school improvement. Our endorsement of site-based management revolves around the simple idea that members of a school council should not serve to promote their own interests, but to act unselfishly in behalf of the students whose needs they attempt to understand. The Consortium for Policy Research in Education concluded that school-based management "turns out to be rather meaningless unless it is part of a focused, even passionate, quest for school improvement."[86] ∎

The learning goals that a high school sets for its students should drive the fiscal process, determining both the purposes of expenditures and the amounts of money spent. Government at the local, state, and federal levels is responsible for providing adequate resources so that schools may realize these learning goals. Furthermore, government should distribute funds equitably so as to recognize the varying needs of particular communities and individual students.

chapter ten
RESOURCES
Providing for Sufficiency

1. Sufficiency of funding for education will be the top priority of state fiscal policy.

2. New programs mandated for high schools will be restricted to those that support learning objectives identified in national goals or endorsed by district and state policies. Furthermore, programs mandated by government should be fully funded from the level at which the mandate originates.

3. The agencies responsible for education at the local, intermediate, state, and federal levels will emphasize service to the individual schools.

4. Schools will go beyond regular, official funding sources to seek out supplemental resources wherever possible.

5. Decisions regarding budget and staff allocations will be made at the site level, in accord with policy parameters set at the central level so as to ensure the input of those who know the situation best.

1. Sufficiency of funding for education will be the top priority of state fiscal policy.

Since the beginning of the 1980s, state government has eclipsed local government as the primary revenue source for elementary and secondary education in more and more states. The portion of school support contributed by state government exceeded that provided by the localities in fully half the states by 1991–92.[87] The states also act as conduits for federal funds that reach the nation's non-public schools. Clearly, state governments have no bigger financial concern than pre-collegiate education. The interest of the states and their citizens in the well-being of elementary and secondary education goes beyond per-pupil expenditures, however. Larger social issues are at stake in the desire to fund schools adequately. Education shapes the future in each of the 50 states. If schooling proves inadequate it almost certainly will mean that the states will see the burden grow heavier for welfare, unemployment, and the criminal justice system. The quality of life will deteriorate in direct proportion to the inability of schools to help young people shape a successful future for themselves. No American should doubt the responsibility of the state in this regard, a point made early in the history of the country by Noah Webster when he said: "Education should therefore be the first care of a legislature, not merely the institution of schools but the furnishing of them with the best teachers."[88]

All the nation's schools, not just some, need sufficient funds to carry out their missions. Yet, inequities abound. Most states exhibit examples of extremes in funding, districts that provide three, four, or five times as much money per pupil as other districts within the same state. This happens even in instances in which residents of poor districts assess themselves more onerously than their neighbors in the wealthy districts and still lack the tax base to generate equivalent revenues. This is unfair; it is un-American. State legislators must not sidestep their responsibility to iron out these funding differences. A study from the federal government based on 1990 census data shows that despite efforts to achieve equity, expenditures of local school systems continue to reflect both disparities in property values and the unevenness of the educational levels of adults in the community.[89] Legislatures, if they choose, can voluntarily address the inequities whether or not the courts intervene. We hasten to add, though, that equity sometimes demands not only equal funding, but supplementary assistance for those school systems in which students suffer the greatest disadvantages.

2. New programs mandated for high schools will be restricted to those that support learning objectives identified in national goals or endorsed by district and state policies. Furthermore, programs mandated by government should be fully funded from the level at which the mandate originates.

The criterion against which to measure the financial feasibility of each new initiative mandated for the high school is the extent to which it furthers learning objectives. Priorities for funding should be set according to each program's nearness to this goal. The programs farthest afield from the mission of student learning should rank lowest in educational funding decisions. High schools can barely afford to pay for what society already expects of them, let alone take on additional responsibilities that cause them to detour from the main road of teaching and learning. Government at the state, local, and federal levels has grown accustomed to ordering schools to perform tasks for which no money gets allocated, or certainly not enough to get the job done.

All the nation's schools, not just some, need sufficient funds to carry out their missions. Yet, inequities abound.

Education for disabled children represents a notable example of this practice. Congress enacted legislation in 1975 mandating that the public schools educate the handicapped. Washington has never funded the program at a level approximating more than 12 percent of the cost to local school districts[90] and so, now, school systems are squeezing programs for all the rest of the pupils to extract enough money to accommodate the 1 in 10 students classified as disabled. Another example of this problem stems from the requirement that school districts rid their buildings of asbestos. A study by the federal government's General Accounting Office of a sample of 15 school districts found that Washington reimbursed them for only $142,000 of the $30 million that they spent on mandated asbestos removal over a three-year period.[91] No further costly mandates should be imposed on elementary and secondary education unless the body calling for the action provides the money to pay for it. Understandably, school districts must conform with Constitutional provisions because the American way of life requires no less. But the point has come in these difficult fiscal times when other unfunded mandates should no longer apply.

3. The agencies responsible for education at the local, intermediate, state, and federal levels will emphasize service to the individual schools.

We urge central bodies to fashion themselves more as service agencies for schools. This means, for instance, that a state education department will do more to give local school districts technical assistance. State education departments, as well as federal agencies and regional and local authorities already provide schools with some of these services. We propose, though, that government agencies overseeing schools adopt a new mindset, giving greater prominence to assistance and less to regulation. The National School Boards Association says that education departments in such states as Texas, North Carolina, Alabama, and Hawaii are already shifting some of their emphasis from regulatory oversight to technical support. And, in line with this trend, Minnesota plans to consolidate its state department with other state agencies to form a new Department of Children, Families, and Learning.[92]

The Seattle Public Schools offer a local example of what we propose. In that city, much of the decision making is devolving to school councils at the local level; the central office, stripped down in size, is recreating itself as a service organization to support the 100 schools. It is not that regulation would disappear under the new approach in Seattle or in other places that transform themselves, but that agencies would subordinate regulatory work, at least in spirit, to a helping role. Let us say, for instance, that the state education department imposes on local schools the obligation to identify and report incidents of child abuse that apparently occur in the home. This regulatory role would in no way cease, but instead of simply cracking down on schools negligent about reporting, the state agency would take steps to ease the paperwork burden, facilitate the reporting process, and help schools train teachers and others to identify instances of child abuse.

4. Schools will go beyond regular, official funding sources to seek out supplemental resources wherever possible.

Financial constraint characterizes the closing years of the 20th century for institutions that rely on public funding. Those within the orbit of each high school, the stakeholders, must take it upon themselves more than ever before to keep the sun of financial support shining bright. The stakeholders we have in mind are parents and community members, social service agencies, business and industry, and postsecondary institutions—all entities that share an interest in the health of high schools. Entrepreneurial initiatives will be needed to increase revenues and make maximum use of resources. Grants and donations are available from a variety of sources and every high school should designate people to learn how to ferret out sources of supplemental funding and how to propose programs that can win support. Individual colleges far smaller than some high schools already do this. We underscore the word "supplemental" because additional sums secured from the outside should be used on top of regular funds and never supplant other moneys.

> ## No further costly mandates should be imposed on elementary and secondary education unless the body calling for the action provides the money to pay for it.

We do not delude ourselves into thinking that largesse will gush forth. We suspect, instead, that successful high schools will find ways not just to get new money, but to make better use of what they already receive. They ought to engage potential partners so that resources can be stretched as far as possible, advancing this cause through interagency collaborations, cooperative ventures with community organizations, and agreements to use facilities and equipment outside the school. More might be done, for instance, to send students into the workplace, to government agencies, to college classrooms, to local libraries, and to other places that schools can enlist in the education program. Senior citizens centers and the YMCA represent the kinds of sites that high schools can use in ways that promote learning while enabling the schools to save money. Also, business partners could collaborate with high schools to involve students in shadowing, mentoring, and career education. Public and nonpublic high schools should cooperate in these ventures wherever feasible and Constitutional. Sometimes, a school will collaborate with neighboring schools by pooling resources to implement programs that any one school might not do as well on its own. Other times, high schools will decide to pursue professional development jointly through consortiums so that they might get the most out of their investments.

5. Decisions regarding budget and staff allocations will be made at the site level, in accord with policy parameters set at the central level so as to ensure the input of those who know the situation best.

Each high school should have fiscal leeway in meeting its learning goals. Those at the local school level possess special insight for determining which expenditures are most beneficial to student learning and which positions are most valuable to the instructional program. The local school, for example, should have a say in deciding which programs to reduce if cutbacks are needed. Similarly, a high school should normally be able to block involuntary transfers of teachers who want to remain at the school and whose work is essential to the program.

In the Stockton Unified School District in California, the system and the teacher association have auxiliary agreements that acknowledge the restructuring aspects of certain instructional programs—house plans, clusters, and career paths, for instance—and allow for staffing based on subject area expertise and desire to work in the restructured area or school. Schools in Littleton, Colo., receive a certain number of staffing points each year based on enrollments and then each school determines the mix of staff within prescribed ratios. This kind

of authority encourages psychological ownership, but few public schools across the country enjoy such latitude. A study of productivity in American education observes that the United States ranks next to last among 14 countries in the degree of control that individual schools have over their own resources, effectively separating "responsibility for student learning from the authority to make the decisions needed to meet this responsibility."[93]

When a school has a say in budgetary and staffing decisions those in the school will probably invest more of themselves in making the decisions work.

When a school has a say in budgetary and staffing decisions those in the school will probably invest more of themselves in making the decisions work. Nonetheless, accountability remains essential and a school must act within parameters established at the central level even with the advent of site-based decision making. As a matter of fact, officials of the central administration have the right—in fact, the obligation—to intervene in schools that fail to exercise their authority in responsible fashion. Here we repeat what we recommended in the previous section on Governance because we want to emphasize the point: Decision making at the site level is not an end in itself. The pursuit of improvement is the reason for taking decision making down to the local level. Greater flexibility should make it easier to solve the problems of teaching and learning and to implement reforms. ■

T The fortunes of secondary education and higher education are inextricably linked and institutions on both levels must cooperate in all ways for the mutual benefit of students.

chapter eleven
TIES TO HIGHER EDUCATION
Seeking Unity in Purpose

1. High schools will engage in structured and formal communication with higher education to better serve the articulation of student learning.

2. Secondary and higher education will collaboratively develop new and consistent standards concerning college admissions requirements.

3. High schools will build partnerships with institutions of higher education to provide teachers and administrators at both levels with ideas and opportunities to enhance the education, performance, and evaluation of educators.

4. High schools will hire educators who have prepared for teaching by studying in high schools that model best practice.

5. Research by those connected with colleges of education should, whenever possible, concern itself with issues of teaching and learning affecting children in elementary and secondary schools in order to help improve practice.

6. High schools will hire only those teachers whose classroom preparation is provided in colleges and universities in which the teacher education program bears the stamp of external accreditation.

a web of support

1. High schools will engage in structured and formal communication with higher education to better serve the articulation of student learning.

All too often, silence fills the gulf between secondary education and higher education. These two levels of education that depend so much on each other fail to maintain the kind of contact appropriate to their symbiotic relationship. Now, as reform captures more and more attention of those associated with high schools, the involvement of colleges and universities in the restructuring of high schools is essential. The success of many of the recommendations contained in this report depends on the cooperation of higher education, just as higher education's healthy future must link itself to the functional prosperity of the high schools. Contacts between secondary and higher education should not be left to chance. Structured and formal communication will ensure that matters of concern to both sectors get the attention they deserve.

High school people need to collaborate with their counterparts at individual colleges and universities and with representatives of higher education associations to adjust admissions requirements, a topic of such critical importance that we devote the next recommendation entirely to this idea. But when we speak of an ongoing relationship between secondary education and higher education, we have in mind much more than provisions for college entrance. The articulation must extend in a generous and expansive spirit to encompass such activities as exchanges of personnel, joint efforts in curriculum development, workshops on instructional strategies, explorations of technological applications, and even research that can be pursued and examined together. The existence of an extensive system of remedial education for undergraduates at colleges across the country attests to the urgent need for the two sectors to work together in behalf of better student learning. A foundation upon which to build these various endeavors rests firmly in place. Projects abound, with at least 2,300 joint initiatives between K–12 and postsecondary schools documented by the American Association for Higher Education.[94] Now, the two levels must institutionalize these projects and convert them into permanent features of the infrastructure that unites secondary education and higher education.

Toward these ends, the faculty culture of higher education must eventually change to accord secondary education the respect it deserves. Higher education's reluctance to join substantive partnerships with high schools owes some of its hesitancy to a reward system at colleges and universities that gives faculty members little credit toward promotion and tenure for activities involving pre-collegiate education. Institutions do confer recognition for what they call "service," though, and we urge colleges and universities to encourage their faculties to pursue collaboration with high schools as part of the expectation for faculty service in a first step toward endorsing the scholarly dimensions of such activities. At some point, however, higher education must widen its definition of scholarship to include the application of knowledge and more of the kinds of research and other activities that can be pursued in conjunction with high schools, as proposed in the report *Scholarship Reconsidered.*[95]

2. Secondary and higher education will collaboratively develop new and consistent standards concerning college admissions requirements.

The implementation of many of our recommendations, especially those regarding the curriculum and its organization, will rely on the cooperation of higher education. How, for instance, can portfolios be taken seriously as part of a student's academic record unless higher education agrees to consider portfolios in the admissions process? The truth is that policies and practices affecting course offerings by high schools are integrally affected by requirements set by colleges and universities. Higher education sneezes and high schools catch a cold. Just look at how badly high school enrollments in foreign languages plummeted in the 1970s, when institutions of higher education abandoned their foreign language requirements for admission. If integrated studies within mathematics and science are to be widely adopted, for instance, colleges and universities must alter requirements that students take discrete, separate courses in each subject. College admission officers should avoid blind adherence to traditional course titles and pay more attention to course content when they evaluate high school transcripts.

Higher education and secondary education ought to negotiate terms for reframing and specifying the essential content and skills that high schools should provide to students to enhance their prospects for success in college. Right now, the links remain loose between what young people study in high school and what would actually be the best preparation for higher education. Such matters are crucial to high school reform. The College Board, an organization that includes both high schools and colleges, provides an ideal forum for the exchange of ideas related to admissions policies, but we think that higher education must be more flexible than it has been in the past in dealing with issues affecting teaching and learning in the high schools. Many colleges, for example, have shown unnecessary reluctance even to adopt the Common Application that more than 150 institutions now accept from freshman applicants.

Now, as reform captures more and more attention of those associated with high schools, the involvement of colleges and universities in the restructuring of high schools is essential.

Business and the professions should be parties to the discussions between high schools and colleges so that the admissions standards that emerge—and the curriculum that they influence—reflect the best available wisdom about the knowledge base and skills required in the pursuit of various careers. We do not contend that the requirements of employers should be the sole criteria for determining academic policies; on the other hand, high schools and colleges must respond to the imperative that every young person who passes through the educational system end up able to earn a living at the end. To ignore business and the professions in this connection is to put a young person's future at risk.

3. High schools will build partnerships with institutions of higher education to provide teachers and administrators at both levels with ideas and opportunities to enhance the education, performance, and evaluation of educators.

High schools can be no better than the teachers and administrators who staff them. Virtually all those who work as professionals in the nation's high schools prepare for their jobs—and engage in continuing education—as students in institutions of higher education. Thus, an inseparable bond ties programs for training educators to the quality of high schools. The foundation of a future teacher's knowledge of content and instructional theory, as well as the novice's understanding of the developmental needs of adolescents, is set in place as a student at an institution of higher education. A professional educator in today's high school, whatever his or her teaching or administrative assignment, must also know how to communicate with students and colleagues and parents, how to advise students, and how to deal with racial and ethnic diversity. All this comes on top of learning how to manage a classroom or an entire building.

The preparation of teachers for the nation's schools is best seen as a partnership between higher education and pre-collegiate education. If colleges and universities carry out this work in isolation from elementary and secondary schools, the new teachers may not be the ones whom the schools most need in terms of their knowledge, skills, and attitudes. It would be akin to a tailor making a suit for a customer without ever taking the person's measurements. Teacher education programs can best measure the needs of the schools by having their professors work closely with the schools and by making adjunct professors of the master teachers whose main work is in the schools. From such collaboration will emerge ideas and opportunities to enhance the education, performance, and evaluation of educators. It will be that much more likely that professors in colleges and universities will be models whose behaviors and beliefs provide paradigms for those of their students who follow in their footsteps as professional educators. Otherwise, the shortcomings of instructional practice they have witnessed in their preparation will inevitably appear in the work of those employed in pre-collegiate education.

High schools and colleges can find guidance on how to carry out these partnerships to promote the professional education of educators in the pages of *Tomorrow's Schools of Education*, published in 1995 by the Holmes Group, an alliance of universities with teacher preparation programs.[96] This report from Holmes furnishes an outline for schools of education to follow in aligning their mission more closely with the needs of elementary and secondary education. We applaud the emphasis that the report from the Holmes Group places on the evaluation and accountability both of those preparing for work in the schools and those who educate them. In addition, the National Policy Board for Educational Administration is formulating guidelines to strengthen the preparation and certification of administrators by embedding their studies in clinical experience. High schools that are ready to collaborate should make their willingness known to institutions of higher education that want partners for the networks of professional development schools they are forming. This process will be helped by a project that the National Council for Accreditation of Teacher Education is carrying out to identify standards that school systems and higher education institutions should adopt for the professional development schools they operate together.

4. High schools will hire educators who have prepared for teaching by studying in high schools that model best practice.

The professional education of undergraduates planning to enter high school teaching and even for graduate students pursuing advanced studies for continued employment in high schools should include substantial work in the field, at high schools. These sites should be not just any high schools; they should be high schools that exemplify best practice so that education students acquire a touchstone against which to judge future educational experiences. A student of education benefits from a setting in which he or she may observe, be guided by, and participate in discussions with a cross-section of excellent practitioners. High schools should hire people whose education includes study in such schools.

The professional development school, as envisaged by the Holmes Group, exemplifies this kind of place, offering a setting for college students to encounter good practice—approximating the teaching hospital in which fledgling physicians learn the practicalities and applications of their profession. Properly used, the professional development school can be a venue in which undergraduates enter functioning high school classrooms early in their studies instead of waiting until their senior year for such experiences. This new institution, first described in *Tomorrow's Schools* and more recently elaborated upon

in *Tomorrow's Schools of Education*, ideally functions as a place where professors from throughout the departments of the entire university and experienced school teachers join forces to educate educators and to engage in their own ongoing professional development, all the while trying to improve pre-collegiate education. Furthermore, the development school at its best is a place where practice becomes the locus of inquiry. The perspectives of practitioners figure in the research of university-based scholars. What is crucial here is that those who plan to embark on work in high schools see the best possible models for shaping their own careers.

A student of education benefits from a setting in which he or she may observe, be guided by, and participate in discussions with a cross-section of excellent practitioners.

Preparation for work in high schools should meet high standards, culminating in a post-baccalaureate internship. One such internship program, Teachers for Chicago, puts teams of four interns into classrooms at cooperating urban schools, where they work under the supervision of a mentor teacher. Whether or not a particular high school takes on the formal designation of professional development school, which certainly is a desirable option, counts less to us than the fact that the high school and the cooperating institution of higher education embrace the elements that characterize this special setting. More such schools, whatever they are called, are needed for the education of future educators.

5. Research by those connected with colleges of education should, whenever possible, concern itself with issues of teaching and learning affecting children in elementary and secondary schools in order to help improve practice.

A criticism of higher education, at least from the vantage of teachers and principals, is that colleges and universities pursue agendas that are wholly separate, purposely or not, from front-line issues of teaching and learning in the classrooms of elementary and secondary schools. To the extent that it exists, this academic isolation has its roots in the traditions of colleges of arts and science, where research is supposed to insulate itself from the noise of the real world. Thus, professors set out to free their research from the consideration of immediate needs. Indeed, the history of inquiry in such fields as mathematics, sociology, literature, and the physical sciences holds that scholars cannot and should not conduct research with an eye primarily toward its possible use. The quiet pursuit of pure, high-quality knowledge is not to sully itself with a regard for outcomes.

We find this approach inappropriate for most scholars associated with a college of education. Research under the auspices of colleges of education—whether basic or applied, narrative-based or data-based—should usually concern itself with teaching and learning in elementary and secondary schools. In turn, institutions of higher education ought to reward professors for investigating school problems and for conducting studies that give promise of lifting the quality of schooling at the pre-collegiate level. This investigatory spirit that we want to encourage in all high schools, incidentally, need not depend exclusively on links to higher education. Classroom teachers should carry out so-called action research on their own, studying ongoing work and using the findings to inform their own practice. The presence of university faculty members in the high school can be a prod and a resource to such research.

As for colleges of education, they are, after all, professional schools like those preparing practitioners for medicine and the law. Thus, a special standard for judging the value of inquiry ought to be applied to them. Research in education should generally have links to learning and practice. Scholarship should play a role in informing and reforming the work of practitioners who strive to improve schools and school systems. While making this recommendation, we nonetheless recognize that scholars sometimes will appropriately investigate matters that appear removed from everyday issues of teaching and learning—beyond the immediate needs of practice—and that they must have safeguards to allow them to do so. Otherwise, one might never see basic research that eventually finds its way into practice. Who, for example,

could have imagined that research into learning styles would be anything other than an esoteric voyage into the arcane seas of hemispheric dominance and cerebral functioning? Yet, discoveries in these areas have led to fresh insights dealing with disruptive students, gifted students, and youngsters with special learning needs.

6. High schools will hire only those teachers whose classroom preparation is provided in colleges and universities in which the teacher education program bears the stamp of external accreditation.

The success of high school reform depends on rigorous standards. High schools themselves submit to accreditation to validate their concern for quality, though we think the accreditation process—through no fault of the high schools—does not always serve the needs of teaching and learning as well as it might (see "Assessment and Accountability"). Nevertheless, it is clear that education requires rigor in behalf of excellence. No such expectation is universally applied to the programs preparing people to work in high schools, however. Under current circumstances, colleges of education need not be accredited, a situation that we deplore. Colleges of education should be able to withstand tough-minded external review and should meet the standards of reputable accrediting procedures. Society expects no less of colleges of medicine, law, dentistry, architecture, and most other professional schools in the university.

High schools striving to meet standards appropriate to reform need educators who receive their preparation in programs that meet the best standards of external review. Teachers should be the products of programs that offer a rich internship, programs in which tutoring, mentoring, practice teaching, action research, problem analysis, and diagnostic work are done in small teams under the tutelage of highly qualified teachers whose work can withstand outside scrutiny. This report is not the place to resolve differences within the higher education community and disputes between the colleges and the states over the details of accreditation. We leave that to the colleges and universities and the state agencies. But we urge them to end their squabbling and settle on criteria to which all institutions can submit so that high schools can be assured of the quality of the preparation of applicants who seek the privilege of educating the nation's young. ■

A high school builds its success on a series of strong and positive relationships with and among those both inside and outside the building. These relationships start with the ways in which teachers, students, and others in the school relate to each other and continue through the links that the school forms with parents, public officials, community agencies, business representatives, neighboring schools, and others on the outside.

chapter twelve

RELATIONSHIPS
Reaching Out
To Form Alliances
in Behalf of Students

RECOMMENDATIONS

1. A high school will regard itself as a community in which members of the staff collaborate to develop and implement the school's learning goals.

2. The high school will engage students' families as partners in the students' education.

3. High schools, in conjunction with agencies in the community, will help coordinate the delivery of health and social services for youth.

4. The high school will develop political and financial relationships with individuals and organizations in the community to foster ongoing support for educational programs and policies.

5. The high school will foster productive business partnerships that support and supplement educational programs.

6. High schools will form partnerships with agencies for youths that support and supplement the regular programs of the schools.

7. The high school will require each student to participate in a service program in the community or in the school itself that has educational value.

a web of support

1. A high school will regard itself as a community in which members of the staff collaborate to develop and implement the school's learning goals.

The success of a high school depends on its being more than a collection of unconnected individuals. The word "community" implies a commonality of interests and so it should be in any high school. The building of community very much involves the members of the staff. And, on a practical level, the synergy of cooperation ought to end up enabling the educators in a high school to accomplish more for the students than they could by acting on their own. School improvement more readily succeeds in situations in which teachers work in a collegial manner.

Researchers who reviewed nine studies of secondary schools pursuing curricular reform concluded that "nothing we saw in our case studies showed more influence for productive change than collaboration among teachers."[97] Toward these ends, schools should reduce the traditional sense of isolation felt by members of the teaching staff. Teachers who share ideas and engage in continuing professional dialogue have greater capacity to enhance student learning. Furthermore, such behavior by teachers provides a model for students so that they, too, understand the value of cooperation among themselves in the pursuit of learning.

The community, after all, cannot be whole unless the students, too, act collaboratively. Standing on the threshold of adulthood, high school students should be expected to behave in ways that show they recognize the importance of larger purposes and can subordinate self-interest to the needs of the community. In part, a high school encourages students in this direction by offering them abundant opportunities to collaborate. Cooperative learning is just one such vehicle. Students might also be taught, for instance, how to form themselves into study groups, not unlike the gatherings in law school, where students prepare for an examination by dividing up the work to be covered and then coaching each other. A high school that transforms itself into a true community can become a place where students find greater satisfaction and fulfillment. Such students will more readily work together to implement the goals that guide their learning.

2. The high school will engage students' families as partners in the students' education.

Students benefit from the reinforcement of education in the home and schools should do all they can to bolster the inclination and ability of families in this regard. Otherwise, the connection of the home to the school tends to weaken as students grow older. High schools sometimes show a lack of interest in the parents of their students and little understanding of how to form and maintain productive ties with parents. High schools must tighten these bonds so that children know their parents care about their schooling and so that they can, in turn, benefit from the caring of parents who regard themselves as partners in the learning process. High schools, for instance, can do more to send information to parents, to hold seminars for them, and to involve them in the activities of the school. Despite changes in the American family, a new study shows that the family's capacity for supporting scholastic achievement remains strong.[98]

Outreach should be part of the agenda for engaging parents in the scholastic lives of their sons and daughters.

Indisputable evidence links the family to the scholastic achievement of students. Fresh initiatives are essential to ensure that families lend students the support they need. This is a responsibility of families, but many parents need guidance on how to deal with some of the most fundamental influences outside the classroom that affect the learning of their children. Students score better in math and science, for example, when their parents control their television viewing, monitor their use of time, and assign them household chores.[99] Many parents need more information about homework assignments and about the importance of providing students with a private, quiet place to study. On the other hand, two-thirds of the teachers in a survey said they—the teachers—need training on how they might best assist parents.[100] Schools would do well to solicit the counsel of parents about the learning needs they perceive for their children.

High schools must not overlook the desirability of fostering a warm and welcoming environment in the building for parents so that they feel they have a stake in the school. We are impressed with such efforts as the School Development Program originated by James Comer of Yale University, which calls for setting up a management team that includes parents at each school. The management team works in conjunction with a mental health team, a parents' program, and outside service agencies. We believe that parents also should be drawn into high schools as, for example, tutors and lecturers. But high schools must do more than simply wait for parents to come knocking on the doors.

Outreach should be part of the agenda for engaging parents in the scholastic lives of their sons and daughters. Every high school must develop programs that reach into the home to make partners of family members. In addition, schools can enhance attempts to promote ties with families by making it possible for computers in the home to link up with computers at the school. Zavala Elementary School in Austin, Tex., taught parents how to use computers and then designed a system that gave parents access by computer to information about the academic progress of their children.[101]

For those who doubt the ability of schools to increase parent involvement, we cite the work of Joyce L. Epstein, who concluded after studying the research on the subject that "parent involvement is a manipulable variable that can be designed to increase school effectiveness and to improve students' success."[102] Ultimately, every parent, whatever his or her educational background, should regard the high school as an entity worthy of reinforcement in the home.

3. High schools, in conjunction with agencies in the community, will help coordinate the delivery of health and social services for youth.

Since high schools cannot afford to maintain the sort of staff that could meet all the health and social needs of their students, the schools should do the next best thing: Cultivate close working ties with agencies to which they can refer students and allow the agencies to deliver some of those services in the school. Otherwise, the red tape of bureaucracy may prove too formidable a barrier for the students and they may never obtain services that they desperately need. What schools offer to students under this approach might encompass a broad range of health services, referrals to part-time jobs, infant and child care, and, perhaps, even public housing information for those whose families suffer dislocations—a veritable supermarket of services that helps equip youngsters for the hard work of learning.

The need for such social and health services as these is often inseparable from the support that students require for successful academic achievement. One of the oldest programs of this sort, Cities in Schools, operates in conjunction with more than 900 schools around the country. It surrounds students with teachers, mentors, social workers, health care providers, and employment counselors who try to provide them with help that will enable them to complete high school.

In Kentucky, the Education Reform Act recognized this imperative and called for high schools to create Youth Service Centers. Each center offers students referrals to health and social services; employment counseling, training, and placement; summer and part-time job development; drug and alcohol abuse counseling; and family crisis and mental health counseling. Piggybacking largely on existing resources, high schools in Kentucky send students out for some services and make space available in the building for representatives of other social service agencies. In California, the legislature enacted the Interagency Children's Services Act so that counties could develop plans for coordinating children's services in conjunction with schools. Funds were not immediately allocated so that the bill could be fully implemented, but, in the meantime, programs for coordinating services are being carried out under two other programs, Healthy Start and the Youth Pilot Program. Other, more focused programs are found in such states as Pennsylvania, where some high schools have arranged with authorities to station probation officers in schools with large numbers of students under the jurisdiction of the justice system. Another specific area of cooperation in Pennsylvania involves the State Department of Education's Student Assistance Program for at-risk students. Committees in individual high schools address the needs of such youngsters, making appropriate referrals for outside services in conjunction with the state's Public Welfare Department and the Department of Health.

a web of support

Not all high schools, however, have potential partners immediately available. Some—especially in economically-deprived neighborhoods and rural locales—may have to work harder than others to find outside agencies that are ready, willing, and able to serve students. The principal, parents, and others associated with these schools must try that much harder to arrange for the services. In the long run, it makes good economic sense for schools to assume these facilitating and brokering roles because of the potentially high payoff to society. A problem prevented or at least one that is overcome will not thwart a youngster. Every obstacle removed from the difficult road that a youngster must travel toward obtaining educational credentials clears the way for the journey to continue and heightens the chances of the person reaching the point where he or she becomes a contributing member of society.

4. The high school will develop political and financial relationships with individuals and organizations in the community to foster ongoing support for educational programs and policies.

Events in the political arena that affect education cannot be left to chance. It is not only appropriate but essential that high schools become more active politically in advocating for the best interests of their students. This means cultivating alliances to build a broad base of support for the crucial times when it is needed. If, for instance, a school delivers its message to taxpayers only when money issues appear on the ballot, the reservoir of goodwill may be depleted because it was not replenished during times when the school was not actively seeking electoral support. In much the same manner, schools cannot take for granted the backing of the elderly or people without school-aged children. Only a minority of households in any school district actually have students enrolled. Yet, the schools need everyone's support and would do well to court members of the entire community.

Relationships with government, elected officials, and philanthropies figure into this equation. Baldly stated, schools must compete for public funds with many other worthy recipients—agencies for health care, the aged, public safety, and transportation, for example. It is not simply a matter of saying that the schools and the young people they serve merit more support than other essential services. We want to urge the schools to seek goodwill

and to keep their message in public view at all times so that it does not get obscured or forgotten. Ideally, funds will be allotted with wisdom, but those who make such decisions need good information on a regular basis. The schools must do all they can to ensure that the learning needs of students are never far from the minds of policymakers and other citizens.

5. The high school will foster productive business partnerships that support and supplement educational programs.

High schools should single out business for special attention, both because the job prospects of students will benefit from good relationships between schools and business and because pre-collegiate education must improve its image in the minds of businesspeople, whose support is crucial to the schools. When asked in 1995 if the nation's public schools "do a good job preparing students for the world of work," only 4 percent of business leaders responded affirmatively, compared with 44 percent of teachers and 68 percent of superintendents.[103] Schools should give business reason for more confidence for the sake of graduates seeking entry-level positions in the marketplace. In turn, business must regard the schools as something more than public relations showcases.

Events in the political arena that affect education cannot be left to chance. It is not only appropriate but essential that high schools become more active politically in advocating for the best interests of their students.

True partnerships require long-term commitments and involvement that the schools can count on as educators turn themselves inside out to respond to the constructive criticism of employers. The concern of business with the schools, which began with a company "adopting" a particular school, now revolves around large-scale change. Business increasingly seeks reform of the system as a whole. "We have come a long way from seeing school reform as a series of partnerships with individual schools," says Joseph T. Gorman, chairman of TRW, Inc., and former chairman of the Business Roundtable Education Task Force. "More and more companies are now actively engaged in reforming the entire system of education. We have no choice but to insist that widespread change occur."[104]

Whatever other goals high schools have, equipping their students for gainful work certainly ought to rank among the highest.

Students attending high schools will in a relatively short time leave formal education for a lifetime of employment. Whatever other goals high schools have, equipping their students for gainful work certainly ought to rank among the highest. Otherwise, high schools—to the extent that they represent an important step along the progression of preparation—betray their clients, the students. This imperative also dictates that high schools constantly keep track of what business expects of its employees so that schools offer students appropriate preparation. The measures that a high school takes to get students ready for employment should reflect a realistic appraisal of economic needs and opportunities. The priority that parents and students give to job readiness is underscored by the findings of a survey in which they rank this purpose as the most important reason for getting a good education.[105]

Students can learn about the expectations of employers by gaining entrée to business and industry through job shadowing, apprenticeships, work-study, and summer jobs, which the high school should help them to obtain. In addition, members of the school faculty can gain a deeper understanding of the application of knowledge by participating in summer internships in business and industry. People from business and industry can reciprocally serve as visiting lecturers and visiting faculty members. Furthermore, now that business regards pre-collegiate education as a legitimate recipient of its philanthropy, high schools should identify projects and programs that merit the support of business. Educators can use the help of experts from the business world to write grant requests for funding.

Schools, for their part, should find out what they can do for business, as many community colleges have done in mounting special short-term training programs. Adult education offerings by high schools, for example, might include courses to meet specific needs of neighborhood businesses and their employees. High schools that perform this kind of role will demonstrate their connection to the community. The schools should also find ways to familiarize business with the accomplishments of students and teachers. Let us be frank: Business occupies a prominent place on the tax rolls. It pleases business to see that money spent on education is a good investment, a recognition that can translate into backing for school budgets and tax levies.

6. High schools will form partnerships with agencies for youths that support and supplement the regular programs of the schools.

Youth groups and high schools deal with the very same students and yet the schools scarcely collaborate with these agencies—for example, the YMCA, the Boys and Girls Clubs, 4-H, church youth groups, Boy Scouts and Girl Scouts. High schools should begin thinking not only about how to make the school day itself more productive, but also about what encouragement they might offer in behalf of the array of activities available in a teenager's out-of-school hours. In this discussion of Relationships, we have already mentioned the need for high schools to form strong ties with the home. What about the rest of a young person's time—the portion spent outside the purview of school or home? Agencies for youth are potential vehicles for putting after-school and weekend hours to healthy and wise use. One study of how such organizations contribute to youth development found that they provide opportunities that meet the needs of young people to socialize with peers and adults, to develop skills that are relevant now and in the future, to contribute to the community, to belong to a valued group, and to feel competent.[106]

High schools should cultivate these organizations as potential partners, promoting them among students and even linking the school to programs sponsored by the various agencies. A YMCA, for instance, might offer a homework helper program that cooperates with the school to give students academic assistance. More than that, field trips by after-school youth groups can be coordinated with the high school so that students visit places related to their studies. And intramural teams from high schools might compete in an evening league under the aegis of a Boys or Girls Club. Researchers maintain that youth agencies can give teenagers the chance to feel they belong to an intimate group and provide "many of the features that in earlier eras characterized family life."[107] Effective partnerships with youth organizations, among other benefits, may serve as potential antidotes to gang membership by offering teenagers the sense of belonging for which some have unfulfilled yearnings.

7. The high school will require each student to participate in a service program in the community or in the school itself that has educational value.

The health of our democracy depends on students gaining a sense of their connection to the larger community. One of the best ways to create such ties is through service learning, which enables young people to contribute their efforts to activities that are useful to the community and helps them reflect on what they learn from their participation. At the outset of such programs, high schools should define the educational objectives and establish the criteria for assessing the experience.

Recognition of the educational value of this sort of endeavor can be seen at such places as Brown University, where students enrolling in certain courses in environmental studies, sociology, public policy, community health, and anthropology face an optional or mandatory service component. In a course entitled "Sociological Perspectives on Poverty," for example, various students in the spring of 1995—in addition to readings and class discussions—were working in a soup kitchen, tutoring candidates for the high school equivalency examination, serving as court-appointed advocates for children, aiding in the public defender's office, and acting as after-school mentors for schoolchildren.[108]

We acknowledge the unease of critics with the notion of requiring students to perform tasks that society often considers voluntary. But high schools make students take many kinds of courses in order to obtain diplomas—courses in English, social studies, and math and science, for instance. These mandates stem from a belief that particular courses have some intrinsic value in the educational scheme of things. Service learning, too, has merit, representing not simply an act of altruism, "but a duty of free men and women whose freedom is itself wholly dependent on the assumption of political responsibilities."[109]

Recognition of the value of service learning can be seen at such places as St. Ignatius High School in Cleveland, Ohio, where all tenth graders get academic credit for spending a half-day each week working at a community agency serving such clients as the poor or the elderly. The program coordinator leads a weekly seminar so that students can reflect on their experiences. Young people must learn to give as well as to receive. It appears, in fact, that many teenagers would like to participate in service activities, but do not know how to get involved. Almost 9 of 10 young people between the ages of 11 and 18 say their schools do not do enough to encourage them toward service in the community and 7 of 10 say they also find no such encouragement from their parents.[110]

At a time when American unity is being punctured by those who would emphasize only the differences among groups, when altruism is on the wane and self-centeredness in ascendancy, the nation should nurture in its young a sense of caring about the common good and caring about each other. Opportunities abound to aid in hospitals, clean up neighborhoods, assist senior citizens, tutor other students, and beautify the countryside. Another group of tasks involves experiences in the offices of social service agencies, where high school students could garner a deeper understanding of the workings of government and nonprofit programs. Some students might satisfy the service requirement by performing such tasks at the school as helping in an office or working on the grounds. Admittedly, some students act as principal wage-earners or as main caregivers in their homes and might be burdened by a service requirement. A high school can develop a format by which these students use such experiences as a basis from which to derive formal lessons on helping others. ■

LETTING
LEADERSHIP
BLOSSOM

Good ideas serve only as fodder for intellectual debate if they are not put to use. And so it is with school reform, a topic about which millions of words have been written. We understand that lifting words off paper and putting them into operation in the nation's high schools remains the most difficult and important part of this report. Leadership requires that some people have the will and ability to act. This report, like so many others, will end up forgotten on shelves across the country if courageous individuals prove unwilling or unable to breathe life into its dozens of recommendations.

One word, "leadership," sums up what high schools need most so that they may bring about change. Leaders combine knowledge, skills, and attitudes that manifest themselves in many ways. Leaders challenge convention. Leaders stir others into action. Leaders take risks, sometimes to their personal disadvantage. Leaders, in other words, may find themselves *Breaking Ranks* with the status quo. Furthermore, leaders build the capacity to sustain improvement so that it extends beyond their personal involvement. They do this by providing the mechanisms to produce the next generation of leaders. Thus, our final section of recommendations revolves around the leadership that must exhibit itself so that America's high schools will carry out the recommendations that we offer in this report.

Recognition of the need to share decision making has grown, fostering an awareness of the possibility that someone who emerges as a leader may hold no official position whatsoever and may act as a leader only in a particular situation. Leadership in this case comes to the fore as a result of the ways in which people, including teachers and others in the school community, cope with situations that confront them. This kind of leadership is every bit as important as that long associated with those who hold top positions—the superintendents, principals, and officers of teacher organizations. And so, with these thoughts in mind, we offer the final set of recommendations to produce the restructured high school for the 21st century. ■

FFor the success
of school reform,
leadership must
diffuse itself
throughout the
school communi-
ty. The principal
occupies the piv-
otal position, but
restructuring
cannot prevail
unless it draws
on the strengths
of teachers and
others associated
with the high
school.

chapter thirteen
LEADERSHIP
Attributes That Need Nourishing

RECOMMENDATIONS

1. The principal will provide leadership in the high school community by building and maintaining a vision, direction, and focus for student learning.

2. Selection of high school principals will be based on qualities of leadership rooted in established knowledge and skills that result in dedication to good instructional practice and learning.

3. Current principals will build and refine the skills and knowledge required to lead and manage change.

4. The principal will foster an atmosphere that encourages teachers to take risks to meet the needs of students.

5. The superintendent and other central office administrators, as well as school board members, will exercise leadership in support of the planning, implementation, and long-range momentum of improvement at the school level.

6. Teachers will provide the leadership essential to the success of reform, collaborating with others in the educational community to redefine the role of the teacher and to identify sources of support for that redefined role.

7. The leadership of students, parents, and others in the school community will enhance the work of the principal, who should recognize this potential for leadership by nurturing and supporting it.

letting leadership blossom

1. The principal will provide leadership in the high school community by building and maintaining a vision, direction, and focus for student learning.

Can any high school change for the better without the leadership of its principal? Not very likely. The post of principal represents the starting point for school improvement. "Leadership is a powerful tool for change and, in my opinion, the most critical factor in turning around troubled schools," says Frank N. Mickens, who as principal of Boys and Girls High School in Brooklyn, N.Y., contributed greatly to that school's improvement. "Administrators who can provide vision and direction are invaluable to establishing productive, success-oriented school environments." Between 1986 and 1994, the graduation rate at Boys and Girls—with an enrollment that reached 4,300—rose from 81 percent to 95 percent and the college-going rate increased from 50 percent to 75 percent.[111]

It is not simply that a principal sets the climate for change; the principal also must not impede change. The principal should help those in the school community recognize that sometimes they become prisoners to the paradigms by which they view the world, showing them how their responses to problems of former years may not suit today's challenges—and may not have worked even as well as they thought in the past. Kenneth J. Tewel, a former principal at three different New York City high schools, writes of the need for principals to overcome mindsets that restrict their vision and limit their ability to see new possibilities that are essential to changing established but ineffective practices.[112]

When some 80 education professors and school administrators gathered in St. Louis in the early spring of 1995 to consider the implications of school reform for leadership and for the preparation of leaders they settled on three main themes. According to this group of scholars and practitioners, a leader should define and sustain purpose, develop and nurture community, and foster personal and organizational growth.[113] The high school principal, to our way of thinking, is the keeper of the dream, representing the school both to the community within the school and to the outside community.

The principal must display the courage to lead even when no one else offers to don the mantle of school leadership. A principal who leads well keeps the objectives of change in everyone's sight through the most trying times, when clouds of despair block the view of the future and prospects for improvement appear bleakest. The principal helps people believe in larger possibilities in order to sustain the hopes of those who want to create a better high school. This kind of principal can handle the politics, collaboration, consensus building, and quality management on which the school's well-being depends. He or she points to student learning as the compass by which the high school must set its course.

An effective principal must inspire and lead by example. He or she should be a defender of academic integrity.

While some aspects of a high school principal's job are unique, we think successful high school principals have much in common with successful chief executives in business. An examination by the *Wall Street Journal* of several CEOs who turned around troubled corporations identified five traits that might very well apply to principals. The executives showed clear vision, charisma, and decisive leadership; they changed the old culture in their organizations; they tackled many problems at once; they changed how employees were judged and rewarded; and their directors (read this as superintendents and school board members) backed their plans and held them accountable.[114]

2. Selection of high school principals will be based on qualities of leadership rooted in established knowledge and skills that result in dedication to good instructional practice and learning.

If we make no other point about the importance of leadership to school restructuring, we want to impress on all readers of this report that any district that takes the improvement of high school education seriously will ensure that no one occupies the principalship who does not possess leadership qualities. While some other recommendations in this report carry costly price tags, this one involves absolutely no additional expense and is entirely achievable within existing budgets. This means an appointee must already have established his or her leadership credentials or show unquestioned promise of performing as a leader once in the post.

Records of accomplishment are especially important in regard to leadership on matters of teaching and learning. Yes, a high school needs a capable manager at its helm, but management skills in the absence of potential for distinguished instructional leadership should not result in the awarding of a principalship. An effective principal must inspire and lead by example. He or she should be a defender of academic integrity. Ultimately, a principal's actions must demonstrate a commitment to learning and a respect for teachers and staff. A principal should be capable of creating a climate conducive to good schooling.

A candidate for a principalship must show promise of success through effective performance in an evaluation requiring actual demonstration of the knowledge and skills needed for this work. This includes knowing how to work with groups in order to reach high quality decisions and how to plan the use of resources. Moreover, a prospective principal should be able to motivate people and communicate with them clearly. Both the National Association of Secondary School Principals and the National Policy Board for Educational Administration have identified the knowledge and skills essential for effective practice.[115]

A high school needs a principal who is passionate about the learning of students, someone who gives promise of leading others in arriving at a clearly articulated vision that focuses on student learning. To attain success in today's uncertain educational climate, a principal must support teachers as they deal with change and draw out the leadership potential of all members of the staff, particularly those teachers who can help their colleagues adjust to new roles. Familiarity with research relating to secondary education greatly strengthens a principal, making it possible for him or her to draw on examples of good practice in order to avoid pitfalls. A principal predisposed toward scholarship can support members of the high school's professional staff in their own investigations in behalf of better teaching and learning in the school. In sum, this picture of what it takes to perform effectively as a high school principal should provide a template for assessing all candidates for the job.

3. Current principals will build and refine the skills and knowledge required to lead and manage change.

Most of the men and women who will be principals when the 21st century arrives are already sitting in their offices. While it is essential to talk about the qualifications to look for in candidates for the principalship, we must also examine what current principals should do to provide the leadership their schools will require. In some ways, the future holds a greater challenge for existing principals than for those not yet appointed because the ground rules have been changing under their feet ever since the incumbents assumed their positions. The authoritarianism and aloofness that marked the leadership style of some high school principals in years past has fading appeal in the collaborative and collegial climate associated with today's educational reform. Leadership qualities that distinguished some principals just a few years ago apply less and less as high schools move toward shared decision making and as site-based management and instructional leadership grow in importance.

School systems should stand ready to help current principals maintain their footing despite these tectonic shifts in the educational landscape. Among the emergent areas requiring attention are those having to do with balancing resources, building consensus, and knowing about instruction that takes account of individual needs and the latest findings in brain research and cognitive theory.

Principals who have remained above the fray must gain the political savvy to lead their schools around obstacles that have an impact even if they are not of the high school's making. Principals who thought that entrepreneurship was best left to their friends who majored in business will need to show their high schools how to use scarce resources effectively and how to tap into funds beyond those received from their school boards. Principals who thought sound management skills were enough to do the job must obtain sufficient grounding in state-of-the-art teaching and learning to offer insightful observations on instructional reform. It will not be enough for those who already hold principalships to become familiar with the most salient issues: They must reach a level at which they can assert leadership and rally others in behalf of improvement.

letting leadership blossom

4. The principal will foster an atmosphere that encourages teachers to take risks to meet the needs of students.

Teachers should not incur penalties for taking responsible risks in behalf of better instruction. Sometimes out-of-the-ordinary methods can promote the cause of educational improvement. Thus, teachers must feel free to innovate if they do so with prudence and in the best interests of students. This will occur more readily if principals encourage teachers to conduct themselves in a bold manner, especially at a time when so many new policies and practices associated with restructuring are trying to take hold. "Perhaps the most important function of a principal is to help release the latent talents of faculty," observes a report sponsored by the Ford Foundation."[116]

The principal plays the role of enabler, building a climate in which members of the staff can take responsible risks to branch out in new directions. Exemplary teachers from around the country attest to this imperative. They say they flourish in their work when their principals give them license to move in new directions on behalf of their students.[117] A secure principal tolerates reasonable mistakes by teachers who try to bolster the learning of their students and protects such teachers from critics who have no patience for innovation. These principals, in turn, need the affirmative support of superintendents who appreciate the enabling role of the principal.

5. The superintendent and other central office administrators, as well as school board members, will exercise leadership in support of the planning, implementation, and long-range momentum of improvement at the school level.

We have already discussed the role of the superintendent, other central administrators, and members of the school board in terms of their responsibilities for governance. Now, we would like to connect that central governing role to specific acts of leadership in behalf of school improvement. The superintendent, as well as board members and those in the central administration, should contribute fundamentally to the vision that guides high schools so they can promote successful teaching and learning inside each classroom. The day-to-day operations of each high school and of every other school in the system thrive or falter in response to signals transmitted by the superintendent and his or her deputies. Their

support and energy form the psychological buttresses that strengthen restructuring efforts in individual schools. "The school superintendent is usually the single most important actor in the improvement process," researchers at the Rand Corporation concluded after a study of urban school systems that had made significant improvement.[118]

High schools working to restructure need the confidence and assurance that stem from the support of the superintendent. A superintendent who fails to make unequivocally clear to everyone involved with the school that he or she backs the principal withholds a vital source of sustenance for restructuring. Figuratively, reform can starve to death if it does not receive a steady diet of this kind of support. Central office officials should show their backing from the very beginning of the planning process by providing the resources that a high school typically needs as it launches its investigation of change. This support should continue as the school implements its strategies for change and tries to cope with the ensuing upheaval, which inevitably will occur.

No high school community should feel isolated from its central office during the difficult days of restructuring. The school board and the superintendent can provide for the continuity and stability that individual schools need as they plod the twisting, unpaved road of reform with its curves and bumps. Teachers, principals, and central administrators must remain in their posts long enough to see the changes take hold. Efforts can be undone by transfers and resignations. The superintendent, backed by the school board, should ensure that multi-year contracts are available for key personnel and create a climate that makes people want to remain in their jobs so they may bring long-term plans to fruition.

6. Teachers will provide the leadership essential to the success of reform, collaborating with others in the educational community to redefine the role of the teacher and to identify sources of support for that redefined role.

The burden of school leadership is too heavy for any one person, however strong, to bear alone. Every principal and every school gains when it allows leadership to emerge, depending on the issue at hand, from throughout the faculty. This happens more readily in a high school receptive to the input of school councils and committees. School policies should support such leadership, and schools should offer training to teachers who aspire to leadership.

The recommendations in this report imply a need to redefine what it means to be a high school teacher. Certainly high schools ought to expect some of the new leadership to bubble up from the ranks of the growing number of exemplary teachers whose expertise will be validated in coming years by the National Board for Professional Teaching Standards. We hope colleagues find it possible to look to these masterful veterans for inspiration, ideas, and help.

Teachers in restructured high schools will need new knowledge about their subjects and about other subjects in the curriculum for which they formerly bore no responsibility under a curriculum that erected walls between the subjects. They must know how to engage learners by designing work of high quality and using a range of appropriate instructional strategies. They must handle expanded responsibilities for advising students and must grow more adept at collaborating with colleagues. They have to take on roles in governance by participating in site-based councils and by sitting on various school committees. Faculty members who best fulfill these new roles will influence their colleagues. The ERIC Clearinghouse on Educational Management in its review of the literature on change points out that when the principal plays a transformational role, teachers blossom as instructional leaders because the principal encourages and elicits these talents. The researchers say that a principal strives toward these ends by promoting staff ownership of change, developing a leadership team, managing decision making in group settings, and building community support for the school.[119]

High schools, in turn, should help teachers get the assistance they need to meet increased demands and then hold them accountable for the manner in which they carry out their new roles and duties. Teachers, no less than other professionals, should expect to adjust to changes during the course of a career. This has been the natural order of things in many fields. Writers and reporters now practice their craft on word processors instead of typewriters. Dentists work with materials that did not exist when they began practice. Physicians and surgeons perform procedures, some highly invasive, that

were developed only during the last few years. Architects render with computer-assisted design instead of doing freehand drawings. Accountants keep abreast of ever-changing tax laws. Educators have no less of a responsibility to keep up with shifting demands, and the leaders among them can show others the way.

7. The leadership of students, parents, and others in the school community will enhance the work of the principal, who should recognize this potential for leadership by nurturing and supporting it.

As we have just pointed out, high schools will benefit from the transformational leadership of principals who help schools attain their goals through the leadership of others. The leadership of students, for instance, enriches a high school and provides valuable experience for the young people who assume leadership roles. A survey of 600 high school seniors found that those recognized as leaders participated to a greater extent than their classmates in cocurricular activities, including student government, interscholastic sports, and the performing arts.[120]

> # The leadership of students ...enriches a high school and provides valuable experience for the young people who assume leadership roles.

In today's high school, student leadership in behalf of the various facets of restructuring will add credibility to the goals of reform. The Commission that prepared this report benefited from the input of two students—Noreen Nilan of Pompesaug High School in Southbury, Conn., and Sidney Martin, III, of J. O. Johnson High School in Huntsville, Ala. Student leadership also manifests itself in the Coalition of Essential Schools, the reform network that committed itself to hearing the student voice by including students on the panels at its Fall Forum in New York City last year.

The high school years provide preparation for the rest of life. Some students who evolve as leaders in high school almost certainly will be leaders in other spheres as adults.

letting leadership blossom

But even if they never again take on the responsibility of leadership, those who have the opportunity to lead in high school gain experience that will serve them well. Just one example of student leadership can be seen in student publications, where editors practice analysis, critical thinking, and decision making in the process of producing newspapers and yearbooks. They also learn the importance of such democratic principles as open, public examination of current issues, fairness, and respect for a variety of viewpoints. In fulfilling the demands of leadership, students apply the judgment and reasoning that their teachers try to teach them in their classes and in cocurricular activities.

The likelihood of high schools enlisting the support of the community in the cause of reform will grow to the extent that schools truly embrace members of the community as partners in the effort. This means that parents, neighborhood residents, and others in the community should have the chance to assume some of the responsibility and even some of the leadership for improving schools. We are not proposing in any way to dilute or denigrate the expertise and professional status of educators, but to provide them with partners who will ease their burdens. The synergy unleashed by this openness could enable the school to achieve more of its goals. As it is, educators frequently complain about the low level of support that they say schools receive from parents and other members of the community. Educators maintain that they labor in isolation to build a better future for young people. This, of course, is not as it should be. Educators ought to feel that the community supports the aims and objectives of the schools, particularly at a time when reform puts fresh demands on education.

Pennsylvania's Hatboro-Horsham School District held a "futures convention" so that stakeholders could evaluate the educational program in the school system and help create a vision for the future. The meeting brought together parents, students, teachers, support staff, business administrators, and senior citizens whose discussions were led by facilitators. This was the

---

The likelihood of high schools enlisting the support of the community in the cause of reform will grow to the extent that schools truly embrace members of the community as partners in the effort.

---

forerunner to a new strategic plan implemented in the district. In the school district in Phillipsburg, N.J., 10 teams comprising teachers, administrators, parents, students, and other members of the community met for focus groups, conducted interviews, and reviewed documents to examine the school system's capacity to begin and maintain a long-term change process. The teams held a total of 107 meetings, conducted 301 interviews, and engaged 1,628 individuals in the entire process as each team took responsibility for writing a report on its findings. ∎

THE DEMOCRATIC IMPERATIVE

The cost of educating young people is the price of democracy, which cannot be built on ignorance. Literacy and the ability to think and reason are the underpinnings of a free society. Without schooling, young people would find it difficult to gain the skills and knowledge required for pursuing careers. Nor would they readily acquire the attitudes that they need for interacting responsibly with others, on and off the job. "Liberty, democracy, domestic tranquillity, economic prosperity, and all the other benefits traditionally associated with American society require an educated people," the National School Boards Association declared in what it called its Core Message in 1995. "Ensuring the development of that educated populace is the bedrock purpose of public education."[121]

As the capstone of the educational experience that precedes entry to college or to the adult world of work, high school occupies a pivotal position in preparing young people for democratic and civic life. The family, in what it does or does not do, will always be the paramount influence, but young people find their voice and begin to discover their métier in the crucible we call high school. It provides safe ground, where they can develop socially and intellectually, sometimes by trial and error, and still enjoy the advantage of a support system designed to protect and sustain them so long as they act within prescribed parameters.

For all its shortcomings, the high school has served America well. Generation upon generation has reached productive and rewarding adulthood having benefited from the transforming experience of high school. The genius of the system of public education has been its contribution to nation-building. Young people of all backgrounds learn how to be Americans in the country's high schools. This would be a different kind of nation if the system of the common public school had not been dominant throughout this century.

Of course, parochial and independent high schools have figured importantly in this process and we do not in any way wish to denigrate their contributions. This report deliberately directs itself to the improvement of all high schools, not just those in the public sector. We would be derelict, however, if we failed to emphasize in these troubled times that we hope, expect, and believe that public high schools can gain strength and reconstitute themselves so that they may continue to make America all that it is capable of being. Education in a free society is a fundamental right and requirement for all—a cornerstone of American democracy. An educated populace is imperative. Public school systems open themselves to all without fee or restriction and, properly operated, function without ideological constraint.

Ultimately, then, this report is about democracy as much as it is about education. The two are inextricably bound in the United States. Yet, we worry that the moorings of American democracy are being loosened by the failure to deliver a full education to hundreds of thousands of young people who leave formal schooling each year—as dropouts and some even as graduates—utterly unequipped to join the mainstream. The shortcomings, moreover, do not limit themselves to the less fortunate. Among others, more advantaged and ostensibly better educated, many young people often lack a grounding in and an appreciation for democracy.

High school reform must predicate itself on change for the sake of improvement—retaining what works, but finding better approaches to teaching and learning in areas of inadequacy. All too many students are bored or struggling. At the same time that we profess our belief that the schools are the bulwarks of democracy, we must concede that in their shortcomings they sow the seeds that could undo democracy. Thomas Jefferson in his eloquent and incisive way observed that "if a nation expects to be ignorant and free, in a state of civilization, it expects what never was and never will be."[122]

Therefore, the restructuring of the nation's high schools is about nothing less than securing the future of this country. Citizens who are intellectually equipped to preserve democratic institutions and to assume their civic obligations must have a proper background in history, in economics, in government, in language and literature, in science and technology, in philosophy and the arts, and in the other areas of learning that will allow them to contribute to and participate in democratic life. Americans must gain a full comprehension of the duties and responsibilities of nationhood. Civic virtue depends on it. As Jefferson said, it can be no other way.

Ultimately, then, this report is about democracy as much as it is about education. The two are inextricably bound in the United States.

Young people must possess the knowledge and confidence to challenge and reject claptrap of the sort that sends khaki-clad militia members into the wilderness mouthing slogans about the government trammeling individual freedoms. Neither, though, can they be uncritical boosters who do not hold their government accountable. Totalitarian forms of government thrive on the unquestioning acceptance of their dictates, but democracy's health relies on the minds of its citizens. "Children learn not just to behave in accordance with authority but to think critically about authority if they are to live up to the democratic ideal of sharing political sovereignty as citizens," writes political philosopher Amy Gutmann.[123]

Democracy in the United States is dynamic. At one time it meant that only men could vote and that blacks could be enslaved. But democracy evolved. High schools, too, must change with the times. The challenges of the final years of this century call for brave and courageous leadership to make certain that the future is determined by people who understand the genius of American democracy and prepare themselves to perfect it. ■

Members of the Commission

Rupert J. Asuncion, Stockton, California—Asuncion is principal of Amos Alonzo Stagg High School, a large urban high school with a diverse student enrollment. Stagg High School is a California "Demonstration of Restructuring" school and has been recognized as a California Distinguished High School. Asuncion serves on the NASSP High School Advisory Council, has participated in an ASCD Consortium on Restructuring Schools, and was a member of the California Department of Education's High School Task Force.

Frank J. Cody, Portola Valley, California—Cody is the Head of Woodside Priory School, a private, Catholic secondary school. He was administrator and professor of education at the University of Detroit Mercy and is former head of the Chapel School in São Paulo, Brazil.

Curtis S. Collins, Jr., Cohasset, Massachusetts—A former English teacher and department head, Collins is now principal of Cohasset Junior-Senior High School after serving as principal of Dennis-Yarmouth Regional High School for 11 years. He was selected as the 1995 Massachusetts State High School Principal of the Year and is the vice president of the Massachusetts Secondary School Administrators' Association.

Esther J. Cox, Anchorage, Alaska—Cox served on the Board of Directors for NASSP and is the past president of NASSP. She is principal of the King Career Center, a vocational technical high school in the Anchorage School District. Cox is a 31-year educator who is a 1995–96 Milken Family Foundation Awardee.

John C. Daresh, Normal, Illinois—A professor in the Department of Educational Administration and Foundations at Illinois State University, Daresh has also served on faculties at the University of Northern Colorado and the Ohio State University. He worked in public schools in Chicago, Illinois, and Dubuque, Iowa.

Timothy J. Dyer—NASSP's executive director, who came to NASSP with more than 30 years in the education field, has served as a teacher, assistant principal, principal, and superintendent in Arizona and Michigan. Dyer also worked on educational issues in the political sector during his appointment to the Education Commission of the States in 1988. Additionally, he was mayor of Ypsilanti, Mich. Dyer was Arizona Superintendent of the Year in 1989 and has been nationally recognized with the Anderson Medal for his efforts in building partnerships between education and business.

Alice B. Foster, Omaha, Nebraska—Foster is a math teacher and department head at Millard North High School. She has conducted professional development workshops both nationally and regionally on curriculum, assessment, and technology and has been recognized for her excellence in teaching as U. S. West Teacher of the Year (1992) and as a State Finalist in the Presidential Awards for Excellence in Math and Science Teaching.

Pat S. Graff, Albuquerque, New Mexico—Graff teaches journalism and language arts at La Cueva High School in the Albuquerque Public Schools, New Mexico. She is the 1995 National High School Journalism Teacher of the Year. In 1993, she was named New Mexico Teacher of the Year and was one of four finalists for the national honor.

Marilyn M. Hohmann, Louisville, Kentucky—A former principal of Fairdale High School in Louisville, Kentucky, she is currently a senior associate for the Center for Leadership in School Reform in Louisville. She is a member of the National Faculty of the Coalition of Essential Schools and was co-chairperson of the Kentucky Task Force on high school restructuring.

David S. Hottenstein, Horsham, Pennsylvania—Principal and director of secondary education for the Hatboro-Horsham School District, Hottenstein was the 1994 Pennsylvania Principal of the Year and a 1995 Milken Family Foundation award winner for his efforts toward educational reform.

John M. Jenkins, Gainesville, Florida—A high school principal spanning four decades, Jenkins is currently teaching at the University of Florida. He is the author of a new book, *Transforming High Schools: A Constructivist Agenda* and is co-authoring a book on the instruction and learning environment domain of the National Policy Board for Educational Administration. He authored NASSP's *Advisement Programs: A New Look at an Old Practice* and served as a member of the NASSP Curriculum Council and the Learning Styles Network Board of Directors.

Laurel M. Kanthak, Tucson, Arizona—Kanthak, former associate executive director and director of middle level services of NASSP, is associate professor of Educational Administration and Leadership at the University of Arizona, Tucson. A former teacher and administrator, she is known internationally for her work in middle school reform and has served as a consultant to several schools and communities in their efforts to improve student achievement.

Thomas F. Koerner, Reston, Virginia—An educator and journalist, Koerner is deputy executive director of NASSP. A member of the NASSP staff since 1971, Koerner also serves on several national task forces and committees that are studying the condition of American education. Prior to joining the Association, he was a school district administrator, teacher, and newswire staffer.

John A. Lammel, Reston, Virginia—Lammel is the director of high school services for NASSP. Before joining the staff at NASSP, Lammel was principal of Millard South High School for 26 years, a large, suburban high school in Omaha, Nebraska, with an enrollment of 2,400 students. Lammel has served NASSP as a member of the board of directors, and as the 1990–91 NASSP president.

Sidney Martin, III, Huntsville, Alabama—A 1995 graduate of J. O. Johnson High School, Martin is currently enrolled at the United States Naval Academy in Annapolis, Maryland.

Charles E. Mingo, Chicago, Illinois—Mingo is principal of the historic Jean Baptist DuSable High School in Chicago, Illinois. He is a Whitman Award winner for excellence in educational management, and has recently been appointed a member of the Headmasters Association. Mingo, a former district administrator with the Chicago Public Schools, is an active member of NASSP and the Chicago Alliance for Black School Educators.

Noreen M. Nilan, Southbury, Connecticut—Nilan is a freshman at Dartmouth College in Hanover, New Hampshire, and a 1995 graduate of Pomperaug High School. She plans to major in government and enter law school after college.

James C. Sheehan, West Palm Beach, Florida—A former teacher, Sheehan is currently the coordinator of Data Management Systems for the Palm Beach County School system. As an assistant principal he wrote and implemented the Model Technology School grant program at John I. Leonard High School, one of only three Florida high schools so designated.

Georgina M. Takemoto, Fresno, California—Takemoto is the assistant superintendent for planning and development in the Fresno Unified School District, and has served in teaching and administrative positions in Michigan, Arizona, and California. She has also held offices in numerous state and national organizations.

Tim R. Westerberg, Littleton, Colorado—Westerberg has been a high school principal for 17 years, the last 11 of which have been at Littleton High School. He is actively involved in the school restructuring movement in this country, and was one of four finalist in the NASSP/Met Life Principal of the Year program in 1994.

End Notes

1. *Marital Status and Living Arrangements.* Washington, D.C.: U.S. Department of Commerce, Bureau of the Census, March 1993.

2. *Income, Poverty, and Valuation of Noncash Benefits, 1993. Current Population Reports.* Washington, D.C.: U.S. Department of Commerce, Bureau of the Census, Economics and Statistics Administration, February 1995, p. viii.

3. *Monthly Vital Statistics Report.* Washington, D.C.: U.S. Department of Health and Human Services, October 25, 1994, p. 33.

4. *International Education Comparisons.* Washington, D.C.: U.S. Department of Education, Office of Policy Planning, September 1992; T. Neville Postlethwaite and David E. Wiley, *The IEA Study of Science II: Science Achievement in Twenty-Three Countries.* Oxford, England: Pergamon Press, 1992; and Harold W. Stevenson and James W. Stigler, *The Learning Gap.* New York: Summit Books, 1992.

5. David F. Donavel. *High School: The American Walkabout.* Andover, Mass.: The Regional Laboratory for Educational Improvement of the Northeast & the Islands, 1995, p. 8.

6. *Assignment Incomplete: The Unfinished Business of Education Reform.* New York: Public Agenda, 1995, p. 19.

7. Special supplement to *Phi Delta Kappan,* September 1995, p. 47.

8. *Setting Performance Standards for Student Achievement: A Report of the National Academy of Education Panel on the Evaluation of the NAEP Trial State Assessment: An Evaluation of the 1992 Achievement Levels.* Stanford, Calif.: National Academy of Education, 1993; *Reading Assessment Redesigned: Authentic Texts and Innovative Instruments in NAEP's 1992 Survey.* Washington, D.C.: U.S. Department of Education, National Center for Education Statistics, Office of Educational Research and Improvement, January 1995.

9. Janice Earle and Julia C. Wan. "The National Science Foundation and Systemic Reform." *On Common Ground.* New Haven, Conn.: Yale-New Haven Teachers Institute, Spring 1995, p. 10.

10. "The Lion in Winter and the Middle Ages." *NEXUS,* Spring 1995, 5017 Archmere Ave., Cleveland, Ohio 44144.

11. Ernest L. Boyer. *High School: A Report on Secondary Education in America.* The Carnegie Foundation for the Advancement of Teaching. New York: Harper & Row, 1983, pp. 114–17.

12. Mary Crystal Cage. "Re-Engineering: Drexel U. Revamps Its Curriculum to Create a 'Technological Liberal Arts Degree'." *Chronicle of Higher Education,* April 7, 1995, p. A-16.

13. Howard Gardner and Veronica Boix-Mansilla. "Teaching for Understanding in the Disciplines—and Beyond." *Teachers College Record,* Winter 1994, p. 215.

14. American Psychological Association. Draft of *Learner-Centered Psychological Principles: Guidelines for School Redesign and Reform.* Washington, D.C.: American Psychological Association Task Force on Psychology in Education, August 1992, p. 6.

15. Debra Viadero. "Variety of Strategies Needed To Foster Learning, NAS Says." *Education Week,* September 7, 1994.

16. SCANS. "What Work Requires of Schools: A SCANS Report for America 2000." Washington, D.C: U.S. Department of Labor, The Secretary's Commission on Achieving Necessary Skills, June 1991, p. vi.

17. *Building a System To Invest in People: States on the Cutting Edge.* Washington, D.C.: National Center on Education and the Economy, 1995.

18. Richard J. Stiggins. *Student-Centered Classroom Assessment.* New York: Merrill, 1994, pp. 26–28.

19. *Extracurricular Participation and Student Engagement,* No. 95-741. Washington, D.C.: U.S. Department of Education, National Center for Education Statistics, June 1995.

20. *Adolescent Time Use, Risky Behavior, and Outcomes.* Washington, D.C.: U.S. Department of Health and Human Services, Office of Human Services Policy, 1995.

21. *Turning Points: Preparing American Youth for the 21st Century.* New York: Carnegie Council on Adolescent Development, Carnegie Corporation of New York, June 1989.

22. Larry Cuban. *How Teachers Taught.* New York: Longman, 1984, p. 254.

23. Valerie E. Lee and Julia B. Smith. "High School Restructuring and Student Achievement." *Issues in Restructuring Schools,* No. 7. Madison, Wis.: University of Wisconsin-Madison, Center for Education Research, Fall 1994, p. 4.

24. *First Things First: What Americans Expect from the Public Schools.* New York: Public Agenda, 1994, p. 4.

25. Theodore R. Sizer, quoted in *The Paideia Program,* edited by Mortimer J. Adler. New York: Macmillan, 1984, p.46.

26. John I. Goodlad. *A Place Called School: Prospects for the Future.* New York: McGraw-Hill, 1983, pp. 97–107.

27. See the following reports from the National Assessment of Educational Progress: *1990 Science Report Card: NAEP's Assessment of Fourth, Eighth, and Twelfth Grades,* March 1992; *1992 Mathematics Report Card for the Nation and the States,* April 1993; *1992 Reading Report Card for the Nation and the States,* September 1993; *Windows into the Classroom: NAEP's 1992 Writing Portfolio Study,* January 1995.

28. Jacqueline Ancess and Linda Darling-Hammond. *Graduation by Portfolio: Authentic Assessment at Central Park East Secondary School.* New York: Teachers College, Columbia University, National Center for Restructuring Education, Schools, and Teaching, p.42.

29. Eric Schaps, et al. *Schools as Caring Communities. Resources for Restructuring.* New York: Teachers College, Columbia University, National Center for Restructuring Education, Schools, and Teaching, Fall 1995, pp. 1–2.

30. Charles B. Hayes, Alice Ryan, and Elaine B. Zseller. "The Middle School Child's Perceptions of Caring Teachers." *American Journal of Education,* November 1994, pp. 1–19.

31. Ernest L. Boyer. *The Basic School.* Princeton, N.J.: Carnegie Foundation for the Advancement of Teaching, 1995, p. 34.

32. Jane Roland Martin. "A Philosophy of Education for the Year 2000." *Phi Delta Kappan,* January 1995, pp. 355–59.

33. Michael B. Kane and Nidhi Khattri. "Assessment Reform: A Work in Progress." *Phi Delta Kappan,* September 1995, p. 31.

34. Amitai Etzioni and others. *The Responsive Community: Rights and Responsibilities.* Vol. 2, No. 1, Winter 1991–92, pp. 4–20.

35. Special Supplement, Kappan Gallup Poll. *Phi Delta Kappan,* October 1993.

36. *Ethics, Values, Attitudes, and Behavior in American Schools.* Marina del Rey, Calif.: Josephson Institute of Ethics, 1992, p.10.

37. *Study of 10-Year-Olds in 12 Countries.* Princeton, N.J.: Carnegie Foundation for the Advancement of Teaching, in press.

38. American Psychological Association. Draft of *Learner-Centered Psychological Principles: Guidelines for School Redesign and Reform.* Washington, D.C.: American Pschological Association Task Force on Psychology in Education, August 1992, p. 7.

39. William J. Holly. *Student Self-Esteem and Academic Success.* Eugene, Oreg.: University of Oregon, Oregon School Study Council, October 1987, pp. 16–17.

40. P. J. Hart and M. Jacobi. *From Gatekeeper to Advocate: Transforming the Role of the School Counselor.* New York: College Board, 1992, p. 31.

41. Christine Winquist Nord, et al. "Running in Place: How American Families Are Faring in a Changing Economy and an Individualistic Society." Washington, D.C.: *Child Trends,* 1994.

42. OERI. *Student Victimization at School.* Washington, D.C.: U.S. Department of Education, National Center for Education Statistics, Office of Educational Research and Information, October 1995.

43. Henry Wechsler et al. "Health and Behavioral Consequences of Binge Drinking in Colleges: A National Survey of Students at 140 Campuses." *The Journal of the American Medical Association,* December 7, 1994, pp. 1,672–77.

44. Bureau of Justice Statistics. Washington, D.C.: U.S. Department of Justice. Reported in *The New York Times,* November 13, 1995.

45. Robert D. McFadden. "20 Percent of New York City Public School Students Carry Weapons, Study Finds." *The New York Times,* October 15, 1993.

46. Millicent Lawton. "Many Students Give Schools Low Marks on Safety." *Education Week,* December 7, 1994, p.3.

47. *School Facilities: Condition of America's Schools.* Washington, D.C.: Government Accounting Office, Report #HEHS-95-61, February 1, 1995.

48. AASA. *Schoolhouse in the Red.* Arlington, Va.: American Association of School Administrators, 1991, pp. 1–3.

49. *An Imperiled Generation: Saving Urban Schools.* Princeton, N.J.: Carnegie Foundation for the Advancement of Teaching, 1988, p. 34.

50. *Schoolhouse,* 1991.

51. Beau Fly Jones et al. *Designing Learning and Technology for Educational Reform.* North Central Regional Educational Laboratory, 1994.

52. *Connecting Students to a Changing World: A Technology Strategy for Improving Mathematics and Science Education,* Executive Summary. New York: Committee for Economic Development, September 1995.

53. *Advanced Telecommunications in U.S. Public Schools, K–12.* Washington, D.C.: Federal Communications Commission and U.S. Department of Commerce, 1995.

54. Sarah Lyall. "Are These Books, or What? CD-ROM and the Literary Industry." *New York Times Book Review,* Section 7, August 14, 1994, p. 3.

End Notes

55. "West Ottawa High School Teacher Menu." *Strategies*, May 1995. Secaucus, N.J.: Panasonic Foundation, pp. 7–8.

56. David Dwyer. "Apple Classrooms of Tomorrow: What We've Learned." *Educational Leadership*, April 1994, p. 9.

57. "West Ottawa High School Teacher Menu." *Strategies*, May 1995. Secaucus, N.J.: Panasonic Foundation, pp. 6–10.

58. William J. Fowler, Jr. "What Do We Know About School Size? What Should We Know?" A paper presented to the Annual Meeting of the American Educational Research Association, San Francisco, Calif., April 22, 1992, p. 16.

59. Michael Klonsky. *Small Schools: The Numbers Tell a Story*. Chicago: University of Illinois at Chicago, Small Schools Workshop, August 1995, p. 1.

60. *Lost in the Crowd: A Statement on Class Size and Teacher Workload*. Urbana, Ill.: The National Council of Teachers of English, undated.

61. *Lost in the Crowd.*

62. "Prisoners of Time." Report of the National Education Commission on Time and Learning. Washington, D.C.: U.S. Government Printing Office, 1994, p. 8.

63. "Intensive Scheduling—Year 3: An Evaluation of 85-Minute Time Blocks." Horsham, Pa.: Hatboro-Horsham Senior High School, undated.

64. Joseph M. Carroll. "The Copernican Plan Evaluated: The Evolution of a Revolution." *Phi Delta Kappan*, Vol. 76, No. 2: pp. 105–13.

65. Linda Darling- Hammond. "Setting Standards for Students: The Case for Authentic Assessment." *The Educational Forum*, Fall 1994, p. 14.

66. *The New College Course Map and Transcript Files*. Washington, D.C.: U.S. Department of Education, U.S. Office of Education Research, October 1995, p. viii.

67. Leslie Santee Siskin. *Realms of Knowledge: Academic Departments in Secondary Schools*. Washington, D.C.: The Falmer Press, 1994, pp. 180, 189.

68. Jeannie Oakes. *Keeping Track: How Schools Structure Inequality*. New Haven, Conn.: Yale University Press, 1985, p. 74.

69. *EQW Results: First Findings from the EQW National Employer Survey*. Philadelphia: University of Pennsylvania, National Center on the Educational Quality of the Workforce, 1995, p. 14.

70. *Consortium on Productivity in the Schools. Using What We Have To Get the Schools We Need*. New York: Teacher Institute on Education and the Economy, 1995, p. 74.

71. *Linking Education Report Cards and Local School Improvement*. Southern Regional Education Board, 1995, p. 8.

72. *Second to None: A Vision of the New California High School*. The Report of the California High School Task Force. Sacramento, Calif.: Department of Education, pp. 32–35.

73. National Center for Education Statistics. *Two Years Later: Cognitive Gains and School Transitions of National Educational Longitudinal Study '88 Eighth Graders*. Washington, D.C.: U.S. Department of Education, NCES, September 1995.

74. *Evaluation Perspectives*. Kalamazoo, Mich.: Western Michigan University, Center for Research on Educational Accountability and Teacher Evaluation, May 1995, p. 6.

75. Wendy L. Poole. "Removing the 'Super' from Supervisor." *Journal of Curriculum and Supervision* (ASCD), Spring 1995, pp. 284–309.

76. *High School Leaders and Their Schools. Vol. 2, Profiles of Effectiveness*. Reston, Va.: NASSP, 1990, pp. 18–26.

77. *Issues in Restructuring Schools*. Madison: University of Wisconsin, Center on Organization and Restructuring of Schools, Spring 1994, p.6.

78. Carole Fine with Lenaya Raack. NCREL Policy Briefs, Report 4. North Central Regional Educational Laboratory, 1994, p. 2.

79. Andrew C. Porter and Associates. *Reform of High School Mathematics and Science and Opportunity to Learn*. New Brunswick, N.J.: Rutgers University, CPRE.

80. Barbara Miller, Brian Lord, and Judith Dorney. "Staff Development for Teachers: A Study of Configuration and Costs in Four Districts." Newton, Mass: Education Development Center; see also Thomas Corcoran, "Helping Teachers Teach Well: Transforming Professional Development." *CPRE Policy Briefs*. New Brunswick, N.J.: Rutgers University, p.3.

81. James A. Banks. "Multicultural Education: Development, Dimensions, and Challenges." *Phi Delta Kappan*, September 1993, p. 25.

82. *Who Is Teaching America's Schoolchildren?* Washington, D.C.: American Council on Education, 1995.

83. *Tomorrow's Schools of Education*. A Report of the Holmes Group. East Lansing, Mich.: The Holmes Group,1995, p. 46.

84. Jacqueline P. Danzberger. "Governing the Nation's Schools: The Case for Restructuring Local School Boards." *Phi Delta Kappan*, January 1994, pp. 367–73.

85. *School-Based Management: Strategies for Success*. New Brunswick, N.J.: Rutgers University, CPRE, pp. 7–8.

86. Priscilla Wohlstetter and L. Susan Albers Mohrman. "School-Based Management: Promise and Process." New Brunswick, N.J.: Rutgers University, CPRE, p.1.

87. *Common Core of Data. National Public Education Financial Survey*. Washington, D.C.: U.S. Department of Education, National Center for Education Statistics, 1995.

88. Noah Webster. "On the Education of Youth in America" (1790). In E*ssays on Education in the Early Republic*, edited by Frederick Rudolph. Cambridge, Mass.: Harvard University Press, 1965, p. 64.

89. U.S. Department of Education. *Disparities in Public School District Spending*, 1989–90. Washington, D.C.: U.S. Government Printing Office, June 1995.

90. *Education Budget Alert, Fiscal Year 1996*. Washington D.C.: Committee for Education Funding, 1995.

91. National School Boards. In testimony before the U.S. Congress on January 5, 1995.

92. Del Stover. "State Education Agencies Reinventing Themselves." *School Board News*. Alexandria, Va.: National School Boards Association, August 8, 1995, p. 3.

93. Consortium on Productivity in the Schools. U*sing What We Have To Get the Schools We Need*. New York: Teacher Institute on Education and the Economy, 1995, p. 46

94. *Linking America's Schools and Colleges*. Washington, D.C.: American Association for Higher Education, 1995.

95. Ernest L. Boyer. *Scholarship Reconsidered*. Princeton, N.J.: Carnegie Foundation for the Advancement of Teaching, 1990.

96. *Tomorrow's Schools of Education*. A Report of the Holmes Group. East Lansing, Mich.: The Holmes Group,1995.

97. Ronald D. Anderson. "Curriculum Reform: Dilemmas and Promise." *Phi Delta Kappan*, September 1995, p. 35.

98. David W. Grissmer et al. *Student Achievement and the Changing American Family*. Santa Monica, Calif.: Rand, 1994.

99. Gregory Byrne. "Study Suggests There's No Place Like Home for Math and Science." From Longitudinal Study of American Youth. In *Education Week*, March 1, 1995, p. 8.

100. Lori Connors and Joyce Epstein. *Taking Stock: Views of Teachers, Parents, and Students on School, Family, and Community Partnerships*. Report No. 25. Baltimore, Md.: The Johns Hopkins University, Center on Families, Communities, Schools and Children's Learning.

101. *Technology for School Reform*. Armonk, N.Y.: IBM Corporation, March 1995, p. 9.

102. Joyce L. Epstein. *Toward an Integrated Theory of School and Family Connections*. Baltimore, Md.: The Johns Hopkins University, Center for Research on Elementary and Middle Schools, November 1986, p.52.

103. Survey results reported in news release on April 5, 1995, by the National Alliance of Business and Scholastic, Inc., New York.

104. Joseph T. Gorman. "Harsh Reality at Graduation Season." E*ducation Week*, June 21, 1995, p. 60.

105. *Study of 10-Year-Olds in 12 Countries*. Princeton, N.J.: Carnegie Foundation for the Advancement of Teaching, in press.

106. *A Matter of Time: Risk and Opportunity in the Nonschool Hours*. Report of the Task Force on Youth Development and Community Programs. New York: Carnegie Corporation, Carnegie Council on Adolescent Development, 1992.

107. Shirley Brice Heath and Milbrey Wallin McLaughlin. "Community Organizations as Family." *Phi Delta Kappan*, April 1991, p. 625.

108. Dorian Solot. *Brown Alumni Monthly*, May 1995, p. 17.

109. Benjamin R. Barber. *An Aristocracy of Everyone: The Politics of Education and the Future of America*. New York: Ballantine Books, 1992, p. 246.

110. The Prudential Spirit of Community Initiative, August 1995. Washington D.C.: The Wirthlin Group, pp. 14–15.

111. Frank N. Mickens. *It Doesn't Have To Be This Way*. New York: American Express Foundation, undated.

End Notes

112. Kenneth J. Tewel. *New Schools for a New Century: A Leader's Guide to High School Reform.* Delray Beach, Fla.: St. Lucie Press, 1995, p.6.

113. Joseph Murphy. "Rethinking the Foundations of Leadership Preparation: Insights from School Improvement Efforts." *Design for Leadership,* Special issue. Fairfax, Va.: National Policy Board for Educational Administration, undated.

114. Joann S. Lublin and Alex Markels. "How Three CEOs Achieved Fast Turnarounds." *The Wall Street Journal,* July 21, 1995, p. B1.

115. NASSP, Professional Development and Assessment Office, 1904 Association Drive, Reston, Va.; and National Policy Board for Educational Administration, *Principals for Our Changing Schools: Knowledge and Skill Base.* Fairfax, Va.: NPBEA, 1993.

116. *Teacher Development in Schools: A Report to the Ford Foundation.* New York: Academy for Educational Development, 1985, p. 44.

117. Maeroff, Gene I. *Voices from the Classroom: Exceptional Teachers Speak.* Washington, D.C.: National Foundation for the Improvement of Education, undated, p. 5.

118. Paul T. Hill et al. *Educational Progress: Cities Mobilize To Improve Their Schools.* Santa Monica, Calif.: Rand Corp., January 1989, p.20.

119. *Survey of Major Issues and Trends Relevant to the Management of Elementary and Secondary Education.* ERIC Clearinghouse on Educational Management, September 1993, p. 16.

120. "Voices from the Future: Students Speak Out on America's Emerging Leadership Crisis." Survey for the NASSP by Sylvan Learning Centers, Columbia, Md., March 1994.

121. School Board News, Statement issued by the Board of Directors in April 1995. Alexandria, Va.: National School Boards Association, June 13, 1995, p. 8.

122. Thomas Jefferson. Letter to Colonel Charles Yancey, January 6, 1816.

123. Amy Gutmann. *Democratic Education.* Princeton, N.J.: Princeton University Press, 1987, p. 51.

Design & Production of this report by Powell Tate's Creative Services. Washington, DC